THE SAINTS

W9-CYY-547

Icons of light and love

PAULINE BOOKS & MEDIA

Daughters of St. Paul

50 St. Paul's Avenue - Boston, MA 02130-3491

Tel.: (1) 617-522-8911 - Fax: (1) 617-541-9805

http://www: pauline.org

© English edition - 1998, Daughters of St. Paul

ISBN: 0-8198-7008-0

Publisher :

ÉDITIONS DU SIGNE

B.P. 94 - F-67038 STRASBOURG Cedex 2

Tel.: (00-33) 3 88 78 91 91 - Fax: (00-33) 3 88 78 91 99

© Éditions du Signe 1998

Printed in Spain by Graficas Estella - Estella (Navara)

THE SAINTS

Elizabeth Ann Seton

Canonization of Saint ELizabeth Seton, September 14 1975

Saint Elizabeth Ann Seton

The first native-born American to be proclaimed a Saint in the Roman Catholic Church is a woman - a woman whose life paralleled the history of our country.

Elizabeth Seton lived every role possible for a woman.

She was a daughter, debutante, wife, mother, widow, convert, a grieving parent and the founder of the first congregation of women religious in America, the Sisters of Charity.

Canonized in Rome in 1975, she brought honor and distinction to the city of her birth.

On the eve of her canonization, Terence Cardinal Cooke, then Archbishop of New York, wrote:

**In Elizabeth Ann Seton we have a Saint
for our times;
In Elizabeth Ann Seton we have a woman of faith
for a time of doubt and uncertainty;
In Elizabeth Ann Seton we have a woman of love
for a time of coldness and division;
In Elizabeth Ann Seton we have a woman of hope
for a time of crisis and discouragement;
Thanks be to God for this saintly daughter of New York,
for this valiant woman of God's Church!**

*Thousands gather in Saint Peter's Square for the Canonization
of the first native-born American Saint*

Trinity Church at Broadway and Wall Street, New York City.
Elizabeth Seton attended the original Church which was destroyed by fire

Filicchis, William's friends and business associates. Here she was introduced to Catholicism and one year after her return to America, Elizabeth Seton was received into the Catholic Church in St Peter's Church on Barclay Street. Her conversion alienated her from her family and friends, making it all the more difficult to support her five children.

In 1808, Elizabeth Seton was invited to start a school in Baltimore, Maryland. Sadly, she left New York, the city of her birth, and sailed for Baltimore. There, she opened a school on Paca Street and within a year took vows as a religious. Soon other young women joined her to become the first American Sisters of Charity. The small group moved to Emmitsburg, Maryland in 1809. Here Elizabeth Seton, now Mother Seton, opened St. Joseph's Academy. The revenue from this school enabled the sisters to educate poor country children.

In the valley in Emmitsburg, the spiritual daughters of Saint Elizabeth Seton increased in numbers. In 1814, she sent three sisters to an orphanage in Philadelphia. Later in 1817 three sisters went to her own New York City to open an orphanage on Prince Street.

The young Elizabeth Bayley, painting by Joseph Dawley

On August 28, 1774, even as the delegates to the First Continental Congress passed through New York City, a little girl, destined to become the first native-born American canonized Saint, was born. Her parents, Dr Richard and Catherine Bayley, named their daughter Elizabeth Ann.

When she was nineteen, Elizabeth Bayley married William Magee Seton. The marriage united two families prominent in the history of the City of New York. Elizabeth and William Seton had five children. As a young wife and mother, devout member of the Episcopal Church, Elizabeth joined with other young matrons in service to the poor, especially widows and orphans. She and her sister-in-law, Rebecca Seton, became known as the "Protestant Sisters of Charity".

The deaths of both William Seton Sr., and Dr Bayley, followed by severe financial problems, strained the already frail health of Elizabeth's beloved William. A voyage to Italy, taken with the hope of restoring his health, resulted rather in his death, leaving Elizabeth at twenty-nine years old, a widow with five children.

After William's burial, Elizabeth and Annina, her oldest daughter, were received into the home of the

Shrine of Saint Elizabeth Seton on State Street at Battery Park in New York City. Elizabeth, William Seton and their children lived in this house before sailing for Italy in 1803.

Baltimore, Emmitsburg, Philadelphia and New York were but the first among cities to be served by Elizabeth Seton's Sisters of Charity. Foundations were to be made in Convent Station, New Jersey; Cincinnati, Ohio; Greensburg, Pennsylvania and Halifax, Nova Scotia. Today, Sisters of Charity may be found throughout the United States and Canada and in mission countries around the world. They opened schools, orphanages and hospitals.

Today, they continue in these ministries, but, responding to contemporary needs, they care for AIDS patients, provide shelters for the homeless, homes for abused women and children, and programs for those afflicted with substance abuse. Wherever there is a need, Elizabeth Seton's daughters may be found.

Loving Daughter

During the long periods when Dr. Bayley was away, frequently more than a year at a time, Betty Ann was sad. She learned during these times, however, to turn to God and find solace in the realization that He was her Father. As she matured, her faith and love of God increased in proportion to her loneliness.

When Richard Bayley returned, Eliza welcomed him home lovingly. They made up for lost time as she shared with him all she had been reading. Finally came the day when she shared the greatest secret ever - she was in love with the handsome William Seton. To her relief, her father approved of her choice.

Settling in

Dr Bayley gradually settled down in New York. He had become known as a scholarly researcher, a brilliant physician and a skilled surgeon. He taught anatomy and surgery at King's College (now Columbia). His greatest satisfaction came, however, when he was appointed the first Physician of the Port of New York. Now he gave himself wholeheartedly to the sick immigrants in New York. His devotion to these poor people sparked a kindred fire in the heart of Elizabeth who had already begun her own apostolate to the poor in the City.

Bayley's absences now were brief - perhaps a week at a time to Albany to report on his work or to present a plan for a new health facility. Even then Elizabeth managed to write to him to assure him of her thoughts and her love:

> *"Should you be, in your retirement, unoccupied by the cares and solicitudes which generally accompany you, a letter from your daughter will be very acceptable. If otherwise, it will be read in haste, and the idea 'Bette is a goose' will pass your mind. I send it to take its chance, hoping as the children say, it may find you well as I am the same."*

Again we see the light-hearted and playful Elizabeth writing to show concern and to amuse the one she loves. Another letter she wrote with pride:

The relationship between father and daughter is very special. It is the father/child relationship enhanced and strengthend by the male/female sensitivity one to the other. In the case of the bond between Dr. Richard Bayley and his daughter, Elizabeth, there was the added factor of a motherless child - a child whose loving nature yearned for the attention and the affection of a mother.

Richard Bayley loved his children but he was a man driven by a profession for which he sacrificed home and family. Trips back and forth to England to study under famous doctors brought skill and fame to this ambitious man, but it was to the detriment of his family, especially to the daughters of his first marriage. The marvel is that despite his long periods of absence, there was always a special relationship between Richard Bayley and his Eliza.

Her Father's Daughter

The father recognized in his daughter many of his own traits: determination, impulsiveness, outbursts of temper, but also a steadfastness to any cause that inspired her. At one time he cautioned her: "...Calm that glowing in your soul, that small emulation of your chest, for a more temperate climate. Impressions in that case will be less readily admitted, but their effects will last long." He was also aware of her intelligence and eagerness to learn. Whenever possible, Dr. Bayley directed her reading, making his own library available to her as she matured.

On her part, Elizabeth responded eagerly to his attentions. As a student in Madame Pompelion's exclusive school, she would finish an assignment quickly, then watch to see her father passing on his way to visit patients. She would then run out, embrace him and return to class.

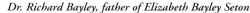

Dr. Richard Bayley, father of Elizabeth Bayley Seton

"I had the pleasure to hear Mr. Delmas, a French physician, refer to... the Monitor as the best thing written on the subject of yellow fever and as the only one that points out its true cause and origin. He said he did not know who was the author, but he must be the best friend of humanity and should be considered by the Americans as their best advisor. I imagine my eyes were larger and blacker at that moment than usual." (The Monitor was Dr. Bayley's paper.)

For many years it had been evident that all was not well between Dr. Bayley and his second wife. Finally, they separated. Elizabeth speaks in letters with great delicacy of "the family situation". Their personal relationship deepened as he turned more and more to Elizabeth and her growing family.

In New York, the plight of immigrants remained pitiful and Dr. Bayley worked long hours in efforts to relieve their suffering. One comfort he allowed himself was to steal away for an hour or so to drop into Elizabeth's home for a brief respite with a cup of tea or simply to relax as his Eliza played a favorite tune on the piano.

Grandchildren

Dr. Bayley loved his grandchildren and took delight in playing with them. Ironically he was able to spend more time with them than he had spent with Elizabeth at their age. His presence in her home was a great joy for her however, recompense perhaps for the days he had been absent.

Elizabeth's third pregnancy was difficult and at the birth mother and child nearly died. Dr. Bayley saved both lives, literally breathing life into baby Richard's lungs. The bonds between father and daughter once more, were strengthened.

In the summer of 1801, Elizabeth Seton and her children stayed with Grandpa Bayley on Staten Island. He was overjoyed to have them with him, though his hours were mostly spent at the quarantine station. The yellow fever was worse than ever that summer and Elizabeth's fears were realized when her father was stricken. She sent her three children to relatives, keeping only the baby Catherine with her.

Final Days

Elizabeth did all in her power to nurse her father back to health. Meanwhile, her concern was as much for his soul as for his body. Richard Bayley was a man of science. Religion had played little part in his life. He did not share her deep religious convictions.

The story is told that in a desperate attempt to save his soul, Elizabeth held up her baby, Kit, and offered this innocent child in exchange for Bayley's soul. It was an incredible act of faith in God and love for her father.

God heard her prayer, did not take the child, but before he died, his hand in hers, her father repeated, "My Christ Jesus, have mercy on me."

Dr. Bayley's daughter grieved deeply but as she resumed the duties of wife and mother, she shed no tears but she confided to Rebecca, her soul's sister:

> *"My tears are dry. They are left with all the agonies that occasioned them, on the garret floor at Staten Island."*

Battery Park, Old New York City, site of Elizabeth Seton's home

Elizabeth Ann Seton
Troubled Teenager

Betty Ann Bayley had a troubled childhood. She lost her mother at the age of three and one year later her baby sister Kitty. How aware of her loss was this four year old? Aware and mature enough to explain why she didn't cry - "Kitty is gone up to heaven - I wish I could go too, with mama." Betty Ann grieved that she was left behind. Losing loved ones to death was to follow Elizebeth Seton all her life - and always her deepest sorrow was that she could not go with them.

FATHER'S ABSENCE

The death of loved ones was not the only sorrow in Betty's childhood. Separation and an absence of love were equally painful for the little girl. Dr. Richard Bayley's second marriage produced seven children, but little happiness for himself or the two little girls of his first marriage. Charlotte Barclay Bayley, his second wife, was a good woman but failed to provide the kind of mother's love Mary and Betty Ann needed, especially the latter, a very sensitive child. Nonetheless, speaking years later of her stepmother, Elizabeth was generous: "...She learnt me the twenty-second Psalm... and all life through, it has been my favorite Psalm." Elizabeth carefully avoided mention of Mama Charlotte's lack of affection.

But what of her father whom she dearly loved? There is no doubt of Dr. Bayley's love and concern for his children. However, burdened as he was with the responsibilities of his medical profession, he was frequently absent from home. It was only when Betty was eight years old that her father decided to do something about the unfortunate situation in which they lived. Exactly what prompted his action is not known, but he suddenly sent Mary and Betty to live with his brother William in New Rochelle. From this time forward the two children spent long periods of time at Uncle Will's.

Indeed, until her marriage in 1794, Elizabeth's life was spent at her father's home in New York, at Uncle Will's in New Rochelle, her aunt's in Staten Island and then, after Mary's marriage in 1790, in Mary's home. And so between the ages of eight and nineteen years, a time critical in the life of an adolescent, Elizabeth Bayley was shifted from house to house.

Pell House in New Rochelle, where Elizabeth Ann Bayley spent many years at her Uncle Will's

Elizabeth Ann Seton
TROUBLED TEENAGER

St. Andrew's Episcopal Church on Staten Island, New York where Elizabeth Seton's grandfather, Rev. Richard Charlton was rector

age of four, Elizabeth had wholeheartedly accepted the reality of heaven and of a God who loved her. Now little by little she seems to have grown in that certainty. During the early days in the New Rochelle countryside, Elizabeth responded to nature as a link to the God she already claimed:

"Every little leaf and flower, or insect, animal, shades of clouds, or waving trees were objects of vacant unconnected thoughts of God and heaven."

And later:

"Fourteen years - at Uncle Bill's in New Rochelle, again... Joy in God that He was my Father. Insisting that He should not forsake me - my father away and perhaps dead, but God was my Father, and I quite independent of whatever might happen."

Dark Days

What faith and love in one so young! The lonely, troubled little girl slowly developed into a deeply spiritual young woman. But, in spite of this basic belief and trust, there were dark days - so dark indeed that years later, Elizabeth confessed to a temptation to self-destruction when she was seventeen years old. The exact cause she did not reveal - only the horror she experienced at the thought that she had lost hope in the God she loved. She spoke later of "...the praise and thanks of excessive joy not to have done the horrid deed, the thousand promises of eternal gratitude."

Finally at home

To be sure, not all days were sad. Living at Uncle Will's with young cousins provided lots of fun and youthful pleasures - but always there was the basic lack of a permanent, secure home. Little wonder that a year after her marriage when she and William Seton moved into their own home, Elizabeth wrote:

"My own home at twenty - the world - that and heaven too - quite impossible."

How obvious is it from this reaction of the young bride that the childhood struggles left only the indelible mark of gratitude and wonder for what came to be. The neglected child came to be the beloved bride - the faith-filled woman.

She was often lonely, frequently bewildered by her father's seeming neglect and always yearning for love and understanding. In today's world she would be considered a psychologically deprived youngster. It is easy to imagine her thoughts: - Why was Mama Charlotte so cold to her - why did papa leave her at Uncle Will's and stay away as long as a year without even writing to her - why - why - why?

Seed Sown

But as Sister Rose Marie Laverty pointed out in "Loom of Many Threads", "this is the way in which God worked to mold the character and to form the soul of Elizabeth Bayley for the great work He had in store for her." Such seemed to be the case. Even at the

Elizabeth was immediately impressed with this "older" and worldly gentleman. She made little secret of her attraction to him. William, on the other hand, though interested, moved more slowly in his pursuit of the vivacious Miss Bayley, but woo her he did.

The environment of New York in the nineties proved perfect for a fairyland courtship. George Washington, President of the United States, was in residence with his wife. This alone set the tone for the social life of the New York aristocracy in which the Seton family was prominent.

The young couple loved both theatre and dancing. They frequented the John Street Theatre on Nassau Street between John Street and Maiden Lane. Attending the balls and socials of New York society, Betty Bayley and William Seton were a handsome couple.

The Courting

It was in the winter of 1790-91 that Elizabeth Bayley met William Magee Seton. She was sixteen. He was twenty-two. Betty Ann or Eliza, as she was called by family and friends, was petite, beautiful and fun-loving. William was already an experienced, sophisticated and very handsome man.

Educated in England, William Seton had spent four years on the Continent making friends with many who would become both business associates and supporters of his future endeavors. In Italy, William frequented the opera, and enjoyed the elegant Florentine society. He had already become a devotee of the theatre during his days in England, and on the Continent he refined his taste for this art.

During this time, Betty lost no opportunity to encourage her Will. There are a number of delightful notes written by her at the time, each evidencing her flirtatious charm, her yearning to see him and, indeed, her love:

"Your Eliza is well, and would be perfectly happy if she could enjoy the society of her friend. I have wished very much to see you... Tomorrow I will wait in anxious expectation. Believe me...

Your Own

"Your Eliza's eye is very ugly but not very painful; but it will prevent the possibility of my going out. Therefore, you must devote a great deal of your time to me. Come as early as possible..."

Miniature portrait of Elizabeth presented to William on their wedding day

Miniature portrait of William presented to Elizabeth on their wedding day

Broach worn by Elizabeth Ann Seton on her wedding day, January 25, 1794

Elizabeth Ann Seton
faithful wife

and another:

"...If you are anxious to see your Eliza, you will find her at Mrs Atkinson's at the piano."

There was no doubt that Elizabeth Seton had fallen in love - a love reciprocated by Will. On January 25, 1794 the young couple were married in her sister Mary's home on John Street. The Rt. Rev. Samuel Provoost, Rector of Trinity Church and the first Episcopal Bishop of New York, officiated.

Marriage

From the beginning Elizabeth and William were ideally happy. Again, there are wonderful letters written by one to the other which indicate both a very loving and a very playful relationship. During a two-day trip to Philadelphia, William wrote twice to his "darling little girl". On his arrival at his hotel there was a letter from Elizabeth awaiting him. He was both amused and deeply touched when he opened his suitcase and found his darling little girl's picture! Clever lady!

Immediately after their marriage, Elizabeth and William lived with the elder Setons, but within a year they moved to their own home at 27 Wall Street, a few houses away from the home of Alexander

Hamilton. It was at this time that the young bride wrote: "My own home at twenty - that and heaven too!" Their joy was complete when Elizabeth knew she was expecting a child!

Anna Maria Seton was born in May 3, 1795, and Elizabeth and William settled down to a more serious life style. In a letter to her dear friend, Eliza Sadler, a year later she wrote:

"...What balls can compensate (for) that quiet calm tranquility which Sunday, and particularly Sunday evenings, affords - with husband shaking his slippers by a good coal fire and a volume of Blair opened on the table."

There was soon, however, a growing cloud over their life. By 1796, Elizabeth realized that Will's health was beginning to decline. She wrote of her concern for "...that health on which my every hope of happiness depends, and which continues me (in) the most perfect human felicity or sinks me in the lowest depths of sorrow."

View of the city of Livorno, Italy, where the Setons visited in 1803

16

Street in Pisa, Italy, where William Seton died

Casa Filicchi, where Elizabeth and Annina Seton stayed after William's death, now an apartment house

The following winter William served as one of the hosts of a brilliant ball in honor of President Washington's birthday. Once again, the young Setons appeared at the gala, a strikingly attractive couple.

The next few years brought joy in the births of four more children, William, Richard, Catherine and Rebecca. They brought sorrow as well in the deaths of William Seton, Sr. and Dr. Richard Bayley, Elizabeth's father.

Decline of William's Health

The death of the elder Seton laid great responsibility on Elizabeth and William - those of caring for Will's young brothers and sisters, and the more troubling burden, overseeing the family business. William was not the astute business man his father had been and this new responsibility hastened his decline.

These were difficult times for Elizabeth Seton. Her loving heart welcomed the seven Seton children into their life, but William's health was a constant anxiety for the young wife. His welfare was her first concern.

Another painful reality for Elizabeth was her husband's indifference to religion. Like her father, William Seton was a decent, honorable man, but he did not share his wife's spiritual convictions nor her need to participate in church services. This troubled Elizabeth, especially as she watched him decline physically.

Finally, in 1803, after undergoing drastic business losses, including bankruptcy, William's condition deteriorated to a frightening degree. Then, because he expressed a desire to go to Italy, where he thought the climate would help him, Elizabeth proved the ultimate in devotion to her husband. She left four of her children with various relatives and sailed for Leghorn, Italy, with William and eight year old Annina. Little Rebecca was a sickly infant, and Elizabeth secretly feared she would never see her baby again.

William's Death

They traveled for weeks and spent more weeks in a quarantine station, the Lazaretto, because the Italian health authorities feared Willam was suffering from the contageous yellow fever. Their only comfort came from the Filicchis, William's Italian friends, who sent food, blankets, etc., to ease their situation.

Through it all, Elizabeth lovingly cared for the patient, consoled and encouraged her little girl with promises of God's continuing care for them.

Shortly after their release from the Lazaretto, William died in the Filicchi home in Pisa. Elizabeth had the satisfaction of having him turn to God in his final days. His last words were: "My dear wife - and little ones - my Christ Jesus have mercy and receive me!"

William was buried in Livorno. Several months later, before sailing for home in April, 1804, Elizabeth visited his grave for the last time and *"wept plentifully over it with unrestrained affection which the last sufferings of his life, added to the remembrance of former years, had made almost more than human. When you read my memorandums, since I left home, you will feel what my love has been and acknowledge that God alone could support it by his assistance through such proofs as have been required of it."*

17

Mother and Child,
painting by Joseph Dawley

Elizabeth Ann Seton
CARING MOTHER

" ...The only word I have to say to every question is: I AM A MOTHER. Whatever providence awaits me consistent with my plea, I say AMEN to it."

These words of Elizabeth Seton reveal more than anything else what being a mother meant to her. They answer the question sometimes asked by those who do not know her: "Did Elizabeth Seton neglect her children when she became Mother Seton, the foundress of the Sisters of Charity?"

Before accepting the role as Mother of the little community, and again when there was question of the American Sisters uniting with the French Daughters of Charity, Elizabeth questioned whether either would be to the detriment of her children:

> "...By the law of the Church I so much love, I could never take an obligation which interfered with my duties to them (her children), except I had an independent provision and guardian for them, which the whole world could not supply to my judgment of a mother's duty."

MOTHER'S DUTY

For Elizabeth Seton that duty encompassed being a teacher, a nurse, a confidante and a guide. It meant lavishing her children with affection, even as she endeavored to instill in them lessons for life.

When Anna Marie, or Annina as she came to be known after her visit to Italy, was only three years old, Elizabeth wrote on New Year's Eve, 1798:

> "The last, the first and every day of the year my thoughts and time are yours my Anna - but I enjoy a peculiar pleasure in devoting an hour generally appropriated to amusements, to you my precious child... May the Giver of all good grant his Protection to you and assist me in my endeavors to promote your future good and advantage."

She continues pouring out her hopes for the little three-year old and ends by saying, "In you I view the Friend, the companion, and consolation of my future years." Annina was indeed to be her companion, her helper and her consolation. She was to accompany Elizabeth to Italy; to pray and weep with her as William died; to learn with her how to bless herself and finally, years later, on her death bed, like her mother to embrace religious life as a Sister of Charity. Her death was probably the greatest test of faith Elizabeth was ever to bear. For months after, the mother, in spite of her sincere prayer, "Father, Thy Will be done" was to grieve as never before and never again.

Two boys and two girls followed the birth of Anna. In all, Elizabeth Seton bore five children in a span of ten years. Each child was as special, as each was different.

HER BOYS

William, the first son, was always that - first son. Elizabeth was forever to have a special love, in his case, a concern for him, whether the concern be for a childhood illness, his education or his independent spirit and lack of purpose. Regardless, the mother's heart yearned to keep him safe and protected, something he skillfully evaded.

Richard was different. At his birth both he and his mother narrowly escaped death. As a young boy he always wanted to be close to her and to William, his brother. In speaking of the boys, Elizabeth was to write:

> "They are two beings as different as sun and moon... Richard always a mother's boy. All his desires center in the farm, that he may never quit her. William is the boy of hopes and fears... and always talks of roving the world."

When Elizabeth sailed for Italy, the boys and Kate were left to stay with Aunt Rebecca. Their mother wrote each a note:

> "My dear William: You know how dearly your own mother loves you and how much I wish to see you good."

Elizabeth Ann Seton

CARING MOTHER

"My own Richard... if you love me, do not plague your sweet Kate. Papa and Sister send you a kiss."

Her boys, though good children and later good young men, were always to be a source of anxiety for Elizabeth. Neither ever demonstrated great ambition or particular talents, and neither followed the plans she made for them. Her hopes for their future were dashed when both refused the opportunity of business experience offered them by the Filicchis, preferring to enter the Navy! This they did. Elizabeth, now Mother Seton, continued to counsel them in letters. Her concern for their spiritual life was uppermost.

In one letter to William, she wrote:

"This morning I found myself praying for your confessor - that will make you laugh - so anxious that he should lead you well... I beg so hard you may be 'an honest man' as you say at Easter, for you know an honest man gives to God his due as well as to man."

William Seton married and had seven children, one of whom became Archbishop Robert Seton, and one daughter, Helen, a Sister of Mercy. Mother Seton's prayers had surely been heard.

Richard died two years after his mother of a fever contracted while nursing a patient on his ship. He had visited his mother just a month before her death.

Her Girls

The two little girls, Catherine Josephine and Rebecca, were precious to their mother in different ways. Catherine or Kitty had been named for Elizabeth's mother, Catherine Charlton. It was she whom Elizabeth had offered to God as a sacrifice in exchange for her father's soul. The child was spared. Kitty was to be the only one of the Saint's children close to her in her last days. Had she been spared to give comfort to Elizabeth as she lay dying?

Her mother wrote of her, "Kitty (my Josephine) is delicate, lovely and pious as an angel." As she grew older and her sisters Annina and Rebecca were drawn to the sisterhood, Kitty seemed attracted to a more worldly life. Her mother, remembering what she had been at Kitty's age, understood. She made every effort to allow her to experience such pleasures by sending her to spend time with friends and relatives in Baltimore, Philadelphia and New York. The wisdom of the mother in dealing with each child is obvious.

Annina Seton, oldest child

Rebecca Seton, "little Bec", the baby

20

William Seton, older son

Richard Seton, third child

After Elizabeth's death, Kitty spent time with the Harper family in Baltimore. Later, she joined her brother William and his family, living with them for many years in Europe. On their return to America, she entered the Sisters of Mercy, where she worked in prison ministry. Kitty was in her nineties when she died.

The youngest of Elizabeth's children, little Rebecca, had been a very frail baby. When Elizabeth went to Italy, her worst fear was that little Bec would die. How relieved she was to find her alive on her return. Rebecca grew to be a lovely child and dreamed of becoming a Sister of Charity. When she was only ten years old, however, Beccy had a fall while ice skating. She did not complain about it at first, but the injury proved serious. When tuberculosis set in, it became fatal and there followed years of pain. Elizabeth Seton once again nursed a dying child.

Bec was most like her mother in disposition. Fun-loving and playful, she made little of her suffering and as she prepared for Confirmation, she grew in the love of God. She was her mother's "true spiritual child".

At the age of fifteen, Elizabeth Seton's youngest child died in her arms. The mother's grief was deep, but this time she seemed somehow fortified - perhaps by a series of events which served as signs that her Beccy was close.

As a mother, Elizabeth knew joy and pain. Each she accepted as gift from a loving God.

Catherine Josephine who became a Sister of Mercy

"Most dear Seton, where are you now? I lose sight of the shore that contains your ashes; and your soul in that region of immensity where I cannot find you."

New Responsibilities

If widowhood meant deep personal sorrow for Elizabeth Seton, it also meant a new responsibility. On her arrival in New York, as she embraced her five fatherless children, there came the stark realization that all was now in her hands. She was twenty-nine years old, penniless and solely accountable for five children.

She it was who must find a home for them and provide for their every need. Challenging - but frightening thought. While Elizabeth had actually borne considerable responsibility for much of their lives during William's illness and financial problems, he had nonetheless been with her. His presence had supported her. It was different now.

She and her children had to live for some time with her sister Mary's family. She had to accept financial help from John Wilkes, a friend of William's, and from her godmother. Meanwhile, she was struggling with the greatest decision perhaps of her life - whether or not to convert to Catholicism.

This was a period of great trial for the young widow. It was one effort after another to find a home, to earn a living, to educate her children - all of which she accomplished in due time.

Church of Santa Caterina in Livorno where Elizabeth Seton assisted at Mass with the Filicchis

Widowhood for Elizabeth Seton meant several things. It meant, of course, the loss of the husband who had been her great love. William and Elizabeth Seton had shared a unique relationship. Their love was expressed in five children. Their love had meant sharing joys, losses and sorrow and his death caused deep anguish for the young widow.

During their prolonged stay in Italy after William's death, the Filicchi family did all they could to console Elizabeth and Annina. Amabilia Filicchi insisted on bringing Elizabeth to Florence to visit its architectural wonders and its cultural centers. Antonio and Filippo endeavored to reach the soul of the spiritually gifted young American with their Catholic Faith. Elizabeth, though grieving all this time, was somewhat distracted.

Finally in April, 1804, Elizabeth and Annina were offered passage to New York aboard the Pyamingo. Because neither the ship nor its captain was well known to the Filicchis, Amabilia insisted that Antonio go with them. She felt it would be unwise for a young woman and a little child to make such a voyage unaccompanied. As Antonio had business to conduct in the United States, he went willingly.

They were about to sail, when Elizabeth was touched by the reality of her situation. She was going home and she was leaving William in a grave in Italy. Her soul cried out to her beloved husband:

Elizabeth Ann Seton
Loyal Friend

she asked Catherine to call on them. This she did and became so close to them that Elizabeth was to write: "Sister Cecilia calls you 'the refuge of the miserable' and is never weary telling me of your tender love and care of the poor."

Of her women friends, probably the dearest to her heart was one considerably younger than Elizabeth - Rebecca Seton, William's sister. They became friends when Elizabeth and William moved in with the seven Seton children after the death of William's father.

Elizabeth and Rebecca were kindred spirits whose souls were united in a thirst for God and a desire to serve His poor. It was their devoted service to the poor of the City which earned them the title: "Protestant Sisters of Charity".

Together they fired each other's enthusiasm for the spiritual. While in Italy, Elizabeth kept a journal intended mostly for Rebecca. On her return to New York, it was a cruel shock to find her friend on her death bed. Elizabeth could not share with her the treasure she had found in Italy.

Henry Hobart

Among the male friends in Elizabeth's life, some were lay, some were clerical. John Henry Hobart was a gifted orator and shortly after his arrival in New York City preached eloquent and fiery sermons at Trinity and St. Paul's Episcopal Churches.

Elizabeth and Rebecca Seton became his followers and went from pulpit to pulpit to hear him. Under his direction, Elizabeth made great progress in her way to God. He helped her focus on her spiritual beliefs and practices and they became good friends.

On her return from Italy, however, when Elizabeth shared with Henry Hobart her inclination to become a Catholic, she met with stern resistance. It was one of the most difficult trials she endured at the time. Years later, Mother Seton was relieved to hear from her sister, Mary Post, that the minister had continued to admire Elizabeth, and his friendship had not been lost entirely.

The Clergy

Among the Catholic clergy, Elizabeth Seton had innumerable friends - Bishop Cheverus of Boston, Archbishop John Carroll of Baltimore, Bishop John Connolly of New York, John Dubois, William Dubourg, Pierre Babade, and many others. There were different bonds with each man. Each one had befriended her and her young congregation.

The one clergyman with whom Elizabeth shared a very special relationship was the young Frenchman,

As a friend, Elizabeth Seton was honest, steadfast and loving. Her friends were numerous and varied in age, rank and gender. The common denominator among Elizabeth's friends was their devotion to her. All loved her as she loved them.

Three Friends

Of Elizabeth Seton's friends among her peers, three stand out: Julia Scott, Eliza Sadler and Catherine Duplex, whom she affectionately called Due. All three women were members with her in the Society for Poor Widows with Small Children. Their friendship is shared with us through letters written to and from each other.

When Julia Scott's husband died very suddenly, leaving her with two small children, Elizabeth wrote to Eliza Sadler: "I have not left her night or day during the excess of her sorrows..."

Shortly after, Julia went back to her native city, Philadelphia. Thus began a correspondence, which lasted from 1798 to 1820 giving an almost complete narrative of Elizabeth Seton's personal life. Julia Scott was one of the Saint's greatest supports, both psychologically and financially.

All three friends were loyal to Elizabeth during the most trying years of her life - especially those of her conversion. Only one of them became a Catholic, Catherine Duplex. In 1817, when Mother Seton sent three of her sisters to open an orphanage in New York,

Rev. John Henry Hobart, counsellor and friend of Elizabeth Ann Seton. He became the Protestant Episcopal Bishop of New York.

Simon Gabriel Bruté. Many years his senior, Mother Seton loved Bruté as a son. It has been said that Bruté was to refine the soul of Elizabeth to perfection. It might also be said that she, in turn, was to influence the soul of the young priest profoundly.

He looked to her, not merely to improve his English, but his spiritual life. Like Elizabeth and Rebecca, Elizabeth and her dear G (as she called him) were kindred spirits. The young priest, like the young Betty, was impetuous and often impatient. It is ironic to read her words to him on one occasion - words strongly reminiscent of something her father had written to her:

> *"...I seldom see you but in such wild enthusiasm of your own particular impression of the moment that you can see nothing, hear nothing but that one object..."*

This kind of criticism Bruté accepted humbly. Their love and respect for each other inspired mutual spiritual growth and together they forged a path to sanctity.

The Filicchi Brothers

There were friends of Elizabeth Seton who literally changed her way of life - none so important or so lasting as Antonio Filicchi. Both he and his brother became her dear friends, her spiritual sponsors and guides, but with Antonio she had a special bond.

Like Filippo, Antonio strove to share his Catholic Faith with Elizabeth. He admired the young widow of his friend William Seton, and made no secret that he thought she should convert. Between the loving nature of Elizabeth and the Latin temperament of Antonio, it is little wonder that their relationship, based on the love of God, was affectionate, dynamic, enduring. Once Elizabeth was received into the Church, and Antonio had returned to Italy, they were never to meet again, but their friendship is recorded in letters - deeply spiritual and deeply loving letters.

Antonio was to remain her confidant, her advisor and her financial security. He helped to provide for her family from the earliest days of their return to New York. He sent her boys to Georgetown and later gave them internships in the Filicchi business.

Knowing his devotion to her and his own financial security, Elizabeth never hesitated to ask him for help either for her family or the congregation. They corresponded until shortly before her death on January 4, 1821.

There were also friends in her religious community, her beloved Maria Murphy, Cecilia O'Conway, Elizabeth Boyle, and others. Elizabeth Seton's capacity for loving encompassed many. Her friendship offered freely and lovingly was a blessing to many, a comfort to her:

> *"I find in proportion as my heart is more drawn towards the summit, it looks back with added tenderness to everyone I have ever loved; much more to those who have long possessed its entire and truest attachment."*

It was the "lived" Catholicism of the Filicchi family which influenced the young widow, Elizabeth Ann Seton, and drew her to the Catholic Church.

Elizabeth Ann Seton
loyal friend

Amabilia Filicchi, Antonio's wife

Antonio Filicchi, close friend of Elizabeth Ann Seton

Mary Cowper Filicchi, Filippo's wife

Filippo Filicchi, brother of Antonio, friend and advisor

Father Simon Gabriel Bruté de Rémur, spiritual guide of Mother Seton

HENRY HOBART'S INFLUENCE

As a young married woman, we know that she attended services regularly. In her letters, she refers to both Trinity Church and to St. Paul's in New York. Once the minister Henry Hobart came to New York, her attendance at church increased. As already noted, under his guidance Elizabeth developed an ordered spiritual life. Her natural propensity to meditation was encouraged by him especially as a means of preparing for the Sacrament. Prior to his influence, Elizabeth Seton's religious beliefs and practices were very eclectic. She now forsook many of these for a disciplined spiritual life tied into the Episcopal Church.

It was in this state of soul that Elizabeth Seton with William and Anna left for Italy in October, 1803. During their long voyage and prolonged stay in the Lazaretto quarantine in Italy, Elizabeth prayed, meditated and encouraged her dying husband to join with Annina and herself in prayer. She even performed a ritual akin to the communion service of her Church to console William. She put a little wine in a glass and:

> *"...said different parts of Psalms and prayers which I have marked... and we took the cup of Thanksgiving, setting aside the sorrow of time in the view of eternity."*

We can safely assume that Elizabeth at this time found Truth in the Episcopal Faith.

Catholicism

Directly after William's death and burial, Elizabeth and Annina went to live in the Filicchi home in Livorno (Leghorn). Here they were welcomed as family by William's friends, Antonio and Filippo Filicchi and their wives. From January to April, the Americans lived in the religious atmosphere of this Catholic family. Filippo and Antonio immediately recognized the beautiful young widow as a deeply spiritual woman. They openly set out to share their Truth with her and to convert her.

Elizabeth was impressed with the Filicchis' kindness - and especially with their religious observance. She had never been exposed to their Catholic Faith which was manifested by prayer and fasting. They had a chapel in their home and they assisted at Mass daily. In a letter to Rebecca she wrote:

> *"How happy we would be, if we believed what these dear souls believe - that they possess God in the Sacrament, and that He remains in their churches and is carried to them when they are sick... O God! how happy I would be... if I could find You in the church as they do..."*

Finding God and finding Truth in a sense may be one and the same thing. God is Truth. For Elizabeth Seton seeking God was no problem. From her earliest days she acknowledged His existence. Undoubtedly, her own mother, Catherine Charlton, the daughter of an Episcopal minister, had introduced her two little girls to God. How else explain Betty Ann's expressed desire to go to heaven with "Mama and little Kitty" when she was only four years old?

Years later, Elizabeth said that Mama Charlotte, her stepmother, had taught her the twenty-second psalm, and that she herself had taught her little stepsister her prayers. It is obvious that Elizabeth accepted Truth in these homey, simple ways. She turned to God and found Him in people and in nature.

When she writes about her adolescent years at her uncle's in New Rochelle, she speaks of time spent outdoors amid the beauties of sea and sky. In times of loneliness, she took comfort in nature and in the confidence that God was with her.

Influenced by her Huguenot relatives, Elizabeth found joy in reading the psalms and singing hymns. Obviously she accepted as Truth the Faith that inspired these practices. There is, however, nothing to tell us exactly what her formal relationship to the Episcopal Church was at that time. We do know that the Episcopal bishop of New York presided at her wedding which indicates that she and/or William must have had ties to that Church.

The Filicchis did all they could to influence Elizabeth. They urged her to "knock" at the door and pray for faith. Filippo went so far as to write a long exposition of the truths of the Catholic Faith and proofs of the Church's divinity. They gave her books to read: Francis de Sales' *Introduction to a Devout Life* and Bossuet's *Exposition of the Catholic Doctrine*, among others. Mostly, however, their lives witnessed to the devout life described by learned authors.

Follower of Conscience

Elizabeth Seton read, listened and assimilated. On leaving Italy she was convinced that she had found Truth in the Catholic Church, and seemed ready to convert. She was not, however, prepared for the reaction of her family and friends in New York. She was especially not ready for Henry Hobart's rigid response to her plans. He immediately set out to refute all she had learned in Italy. He even wrote a formal rebuttal to Filippo Filicchi's narrative.

Elizabeth listened to him faithfully, read his paper, but in the end followed her conscience and accepted Truth in Catholicism.

Painting of the Assumption of our Lady, originally in the private chapel in the Filicchi house. It is now in the Church of Santa Caterina in Livorno, Italy

explain that the Whites were not Catholics and that this was merely an effort on Elizabeth's part to support her children, Hobart apologized and offered to retract his statements and to do what he could to promote the school. Elizabeth went ahead with plans, even leased a house. In the end, after only a very short time, the school failed, due largely to White's inadequacy as an administrator.

Again Elizabeth had to act quickly, vacate the house and move - but where? Her sister, Mary Post, came to her rescue. Elizabeth and her children moved in with the Posts in their home in Greenwich (now Greenwich Village). But as their home on Blessing Street (now Bleeker Street) was a considerable distance from St. Peter's Church on Barclay Street, Elizabeth Seton was now faced with a cruel deprivation - that of attending Mass and receiving the Eucharist. This exercise of her Faith was her only consolation and she suffered its loss.

Abstinence

Another problem was the question of abstinence. Catholics in those days had to abstain on both Fridays and Saturdays. In a letter to Antonio she speaks of this new trial:

"My sister procures fish with so great expense and difficulty (really as if for the greatest stranger) that my bread-and-water spirit is ashamed to partake of it."

Elizabeth was probably over-sensitive at this point, but she obviously was embarrassed and hurt. This difficulty was overcome when the Pastor of St. Peter's granted Elizabeth a dispensation, something she said she would never use except for peace.

On the other hand, Elizabeth wrote to Antonio that she was being subjected to unpleasant discussions about her Church and now feared the effect such critical remarks would have on her children. That these incidents were troubling to her may easily be understood. Having made her decision to accept Catholicism, it must have been very difficult to continue to be challenged, especially by those she loved.

However, in fairness to the Posts, they seem to have done their best to give support to Elizabeth at this time. It is clear nonetheless that she was uncomfortable and felt she was a burden. In a letter to Julia Scott, she wrote:

"It seemed as if there was no escape from the inconveniences and trouble I was necessitated to give the family of my brother P. The more kind they were to me, the more painful was my sense of it."

These sentiments, coupled with her deprivation of Mass and devotions, explain Elizabteh Seton's period of distress.

The struggle to make the right decision concerning her faith commitment was but the beginning of Elizabeth Seton's experience as a convert. She was now to live with the consequences of her choice.

As has been seen, on her return to New York, Elizabeth was completely disarmed by the reaction of family and friends to her plans for conversion. At the same time she was faced with the stern reality of her need to support her family in this hostile environment. She tried several things.

At the suggestion of a friend, she considered taking boarders into her home. This proved not a viable solution. She was then approached by a gentleman, Mr. White, who was planning to start a school. He offered to accept her children if she would be his assistant. This seemed an excellent opportunity, one for which she was qualified. Elizabeth sought Antonio Filicchi's advice and he gave it his blessing.

More Trials

Unfortunately, word spread throughout the neighborhood that the Whites were Roman Catholics and that they and Mrs. Seton were about to proselytize the children. Her friend, Henry Hobart, was the chief source of these rumors. He had already warned Elizabeth that it would be his duty to alert others to the "falsity and dangers" of her new principles. When her friends, Julia Sadler and Liza Duplex, went to Hobart to

Livorno, Shrine of Montenero, where Elizabeth Ann Seton recognized her belief in the Eucharist during Mass

The Social Question

Another factor which must be considered after her conversion is the social question. Elizabeth Bayley Seton had belonged to what might be termed the aristocracy of New York. Both the Bayleys and the Setons moved among the elite of society in the City. The distance between Trinity Church and St. Peter's Roman Catholic Church was but a few short blocks. The reality was an enormous distance on the social level.

St. Peter's was the only Catholic Church in New York City. The parishioners were largely the very poor immigrants, mostly Irish. Class-wise the distinction between them and the parishioners of Trinity was vast.

On one occasion Mary Post spoke of the Catholics of the City as being "dirty, filthy, red faced - the church a horrid place of spits and pushing - ragged." Elizabeth responded: "Alas, I found it all that indeed."

However, in a letter to Amabilia Filicchi, she wrote:

"...They say Catholicks [sic] are the off-scouring of the people, somebody said their congregation a 'public nuisance' but that troubles not me, the congregation of a city may be very shabby yet very pleasing to God, or very bad people among them cannot hurt the Faith... I seek but God and His Church and expect to find my peace in them and not in his people."

The difference between the parishioners of Trinity Church, as well as the cultured Catholics she lived with in Italy and those of St. Peter's had to have been a true culture shock for a woman of Elizabeth Seton's refinement. Her reaction to it is but one more evidence of her own sincerity and the strength of her Faith.

Was there no relief for this convert? Were the financial burdens, the family and friends' continued disapproval, the class distinction in any way bearable?

There was relief because despite these almost intolerable conditions, Elizabeth deep within her soul found solace in her Faith. In a letter to Amabilia in speaking of the Mass, she wrote:

"...The Divine Sacrifice, so commanding and yet so familiar for all my wants and necessities speaks for itself, and I am all at home in it."

She remained the courageous convert.

St Peter's Church, Barclay Street, New York City. The oldest Catholic Church in New York State. Here, Elizabeth Seton was received into the Church on March 14, 1805.

Elizabeth Ann Seton
SORROWING MOTHER

touched her and, of course, William's loss was painful beyond expression.

When later in Emmitsburg, Elizabeth realized that her first-born, her Annina, suffered from the family weakness, tuberculosis, she was stricken with fear, as she knew what William and his sisters had endured. She knew how quickly the illness had ravaged their bodies.

Thus the mother grieved doubly: the agony of watching the progress of the disease in Annina's frail body and finally the death of her child.

Her only solace was to witness Annina pronounce vows as a Sister of Charity before she died and to recognize Annina's acceptance of the Will of God.

Loss of First Child

However, the death of her first child caused sorrow unlike any other. Elizabeth, who at four years old could explain her lack of tears by saying "Kitty has gone to heaven," seemed at Annina's death unable to cope with this sorrow. She was supernaturally resigned but humanly it was unbearable. Of this period she wrote:

> *"...For three months after Nina was taken, I was often expecting to lose my senses, and my head was so disordered that unless for the daily duties always before me I did not know much of what I did or what I left undone."*

Again in writing to Eliza Sadler, she expressed almost despair:

> *"The separation from my angel has left so new and deep an impression on my mind that if I was not obliged to live in these dear ones (the children), I should unconsciously die in her."*

This anguish of mind and heart lasted for many months. Key to her emerging from the depression was the role of

T he loss of a child to death is an experience unlike any other. Motherhood gives life, nourishes the child before birth and after. The very thought of giving that child over to death seems a violation of motherhood. Elizabeth Seton suffered that violation twice in her lifetime.

Death followed Elizabeth Seton from the time she was three years old when her mother died. One year later she knew it again in the death of little Kitty. Later, the deaths of her father-in-law and her father profoundly

Graves of Annina and Rebecca Seton in Emmitsburg

Simon Gabriel Bruté in Elizabeth's life. Father Bruté came to Emmitsburg after Annina's death and became her spiritual advisor. Under his guidance Elizabeth slowly recovered.

Another Loss

Four years later, Elizabeth Seton was called upon to part with her Rebecca. During these four years, the mother had watched and nursed the precious child as she deteriorated physically but grew spiritually. This time sufficient grace was given for the mother to cope. Writing to Simon Bruté to tell him of Beccy's death, Father Dubois said:

> "...The mother is a miracle of divine favor. Night and day by the child, her health has not appeared to suffer. She held the child in her arms without

dropping a tear all the time of her agony and even eight minutes after she had died. Mulierem fortem."

The grace of resignation was plentiful this time. In a letter to William telling him of his sister's death, she wrote:

> "It would be too selfish to have wished her inexpressible sufferings prolonged... though in her I have lost the little friend of my heart."

Beccy's death was a deliverance for mother and child. From this time on, Elizabeth was to commune with her "two darlings" as from her window she could see the two graves side by side. Rather than plunge herself into despair, the Mother now plunged into the work of her congregation.

Saint Elizabeth Ann Seton, door of St. Patrick's Cathedral in New York City

Shrine of Saint Elizabeth Ann Seton in the Basilica in Emmitsburg

put her personal feelings aside, however, and dealt with the situation with sensitivity. She arranged for the young people to meet in her presence, explained that Annina was much too young for any serious relationship but allowed them to correspond. Later, when the Sisterhood had moved to Emmitsburg, knowing Annina was sad, Elizabeth brought her to Baltimore so she could see Charles before he returned to his own country. A year later they learned he had married.

Elizabeth, who knew so well what it was to love, understood Annina's pain and dealt with it sympathetically.

GENEROSITY

Elizabeth Seton was not merely loving. She was giving. Her generosity in giving of herself was evident when she willingly gave up her own home to move in with the young Setons after the death of William Seton, Sr. We recall the joy of the young bride when she and William had moved into their own home. Now, she left that home, she with two children of her own and a third expected very soon. There were seven brothers and sisters of William's in the Seton home - three very young. She admits:

> *"...For me, who so dearly loves quiet and a small family, to become the mother of six children... is a very great change."*

There were no complaints. She sacrificed herself completely. One very consoling outcome of this time of

her life was the friendship that was made between herself and Rebecca Seton.

Elizabeth's readiness to give of herself is again obvious in her decision to go to Italy with William and leave four of her children at home with relatives. The separation from the children was difficult in itself but leaving her baby, Rebecca, made the decision even more painful. Would Elizabeth find the child alive on her return? No matter, William wanted to go and so she went.

NURTURING

A woman is by her very nature nurturing. Elizabeth Seton not only nurtured her own children physically and spiritually, she was to nurture people all her life. She nursed her father, her husband, two children, her sisters-in-law, and her maid-servant Mammy Huler during their last illnesses.

Elizabeth's relationship with family, friends, the sisters in her community and with priests was often based on their need of her or in some cases on a reciprocal giving and receiving. The woman in her reached out to all.

This quality in Elizabeth is revealed particularly in her role as Mother of her congregation. Here her personal spirituality and her nurturing heart are entwined as she sought to enrich and guide these women, her sisters. Here, too, we see her wisdom.

In instructing the sisters, Elizabeth was loving but firm and very definite:

43

"What was the first rule of our dear Savior's life? You know it was to do His Father's Will. Well, then, the first end I propose in our daily work is to do the Will of God; secondly, to do it in the manner He wills it; and thirdly, to do it because it is His Will."

What is most impressive is the authority with which Elizabeth Seton spoke, she who but a few years earlier had struggled to know the way in which God was calling her. Now, as Mother of her community, she was blessed with surety and conviction.

The same wisdom and nurturing qualities appear in a letter written to one of her beloved religious, Sister Cecilia O'Conway:

"The only fear I have for you is that you will let the old string pull too hard for solitude and silence... This is not a country, my dear one, for Solitude and Silence, - but of warfare and crucifixion."

In spite of her own love of prayer and silence, the American Elizabeth Seton is telling this young woman

- a "joie de vivre". How often she used these two qualities to soften a rebuke or relieve a difficult situation. A witty or playful remark was something she used rather indulgently!

On one occasion, Elizabeth wrote to Bruté about a priest who was apparently overly concerned about liturgical things:

"He is so droll; everything must be done by the book; we call him the Rubric."

Her wit and her warmth are delightful as seen in words addressed to Antonio:

"How are you, Tonnino, what are you doing? Do you ever think of the poverina of America? Yes you do and she thinks of you as of her daily bread."

She did not spare herself in making fun. Towards the end of her life she wrote to describe herself to Julia:

"...A poor creature, lame of one leg and blind of an eye, a poor old bit of broken furniture, good only to frighten the crows away."

Father Bruté's painting of the White House and the Stone House

that a Sister of Charity must sacrifice a personal yearning for solitude to the mission - in this case to teaching. It is obvious Elizabeth knew the needs of her country and wanted her sisters to respond to those needs, be they teaching, nursing the sick or caring for orphans.

BON SENS

The wisdom and faith of Elizabeth Seton are frequently seen in the "bon sens" which reflect her French ancestry. She who had been the carefree debutante and young society matron faced stern challenges with wise decisions and equanimity of mind and heart. Frequently the "bon sens" was mingled with another trait of her French roots

Worn out, perhaps, but never less beautiful to those who watched Elizabeth decline. Her Faith which had guided her entire life strengthened with each step of the way as she approached the eternity for which she had lived.

That Elizabeth Seton is a woman for all women is clear. Does this infer she is not a woman for all men? On the contrary. Every man can find in her an answer to his relationship with any woman in his life.

Elizabeth's ties to men, as we have seen, were strong - father, husband, son, friend - each played an essential role in her life. Surely Saint Elizabeth Seton has a place in the life of Everyman.

Can a woman born in 1774 be relevant in today's world? Is it possible for her to influence society in the eve of the new millenium? This book has no doubt highlighted Elizabeth Seton's chief virtues - faith, hope and love -, the very virtues that, as Saint Paul reminds us, always remain and which permeated the very fabric of Elizabeth's life - virtues which today, through her daughters, sustain all that she began.

The relevance of this woman may be seen at least in three aspects - tolerance, service to the poor and the role of women.

INCLUSION

Discrimination in matters of religion or race is a major concern today. Neither was ever a problem for Elizabeth Seton, who had herself personally suffered from religious intolerance in her own New York.

When the Sulpicians adopted a rule forbidding the acceptance of Protestant students at Mount St. Mary's, Father Dubois thought the sisters should follow suit. Elizabeth quietly but firmly refused. She remained steadfast. Non-Catholics were never barred from her schools.

Likewise, the instruction and welfare of the Emmitsburg black population were important to her. Black children were very welcome in her classes. She wrote:

> "So many of our mountain children and poor, good Blacks came today for First Communion instructions, and I have all the Blacks... all the Blacks for my share to instruct - excellentissimo."

Obviously, Elizabeth Seton's spirit of ecumenism and her lack of racial prejudice would surely be relevant today.

SERVICE TO THE POOR

Elizabeth Seton had an option for the poor. As a young wife and mother in New York, she and her sister-in-law, Rebecca Seton, helped to establish a society to aid destitute widows and orphans. As previously noted, they were referred to as Protestant Sisters of Charity! How familiar it all sounds! Translate widows and orphans into abused women and children with AIDS, low-income housing into housing for the homeless, and Elizabeth fits quite well in today's world.

If our Saint had an option for the poor and welcomed them into her school, she nevertheless had the wisdom to know the importance and necessity of educating those financially better situated. In preparing the children in her private school to be future leaders, she also used their tuition money to educate the poor. St. Vincent de Paul worked tirelessly for the under-privileged, yet he expended time and energy to provide spiritual guidance to the Ladies of the French Court. Elizabeth, too, knew that her wealthy and influential friends in Baltimore deserved her love and concern, and that they were in turn important in her work.

When financial pressures assailed her, she found no problem in appealing to their generosity. They were her friends and they would share her burdens. Thus, in a truly American way, our Saint opened her heart to all beliefs, all classes and all races.

ROLE OF WOMEN

Women in today's world are particularly anxious about their role in society, in the workplace and in the Church. Elizabeth Seton quietly prepared young women for their future at a time when the home was the cradle of learning and where the role of women was vital:

> "Your Mother does not come to teach you how to be good nuns or Sisters of Charity, but rather I would wish to fit you for that world in which you are destined to live... to teach you how to be good mothers of families."

Her desire was indeed that these young women become educated, self-confident leaders in the world and in the Church.

Elizabeth herself was gentle, loving, yet firm. She knew her abilities. She knew her responsibility. She did not hesitate to challenge any threat to her authority. She believed that her authority came from God and even protested, on occasion, clerical interference in community matters. Indeed, Elizabeth Seton would be relevant in the struggle of women for justice today!

So again - can a woman born in 1774 have influence on the eve of the twenty-first century? She can, she does!

St. Elizabeth Seton Church in Livorno, first church to be named for her in Italy. There are now over a hundred churches in her name in the United States alone.

View of the castle, the Hudson River, and the Washington Bridge from Mount St. Vincent

THE SAINTS

*A*ugustine

The Family Background of Augustine

More than sixteen centuries lie between us and Augustine who was born on 13 November, 354 in Thagaste, known today as Souk-Ahras in Algeria. Thagaste belonged to the province of Numidia in North Africa, itself a province of the great Roman Empire. Both facts are important: although Augustine's cultural education was Roman, he prided himself on his African origins. He told a North African correspondent who ridiculed the Punic names of some martyrs that he should remember how "he was an African writing for Africans, both of us living in Africa."

However, about no person in antiquity have we more information than about Augustine. Unlike many other churchmen, his origins were humble, and his parents were not wealthy. Patricius, his father, was a small landowner, a dignitary of the village, but a citizen of slender means. His father had to make great sacrifices to give his son, who was a very promising schoolboy, a classical education, which was the only means of access to a political career. In view of this he spent money on his son beyond his means, and was not able to finance his further studies when he left Thagaste. He was fortunate enough to find a rich inhabitant of the village, Romanianus, ready to become the patron of the young Augustine. Patricius was a pagan. He was generous, but also hot tempered and not always faithful to his wife, Monica, although he did not beat her, something exceptional at that time. He received baptism only shortly before his death, at the insistence of Monica. Augustine's father plays almost no part in his writings. Is this because he died when Augustine was only sixteen or seventeen years old, or is it because he was a pagan?

In contrast to his father, Augustine's mother, Monica, played a very important role in the life and works of Augustine. She had been brought up in a Christian family, and was a woman of deep inner resources: patient, determined, dignified, above gossip, a firm peacemaker among her acquaintances. The relationship with her husband was anything but slavish. She could wait,

48

All these events required serious changes in Augustine's life. Although he had to renounce many of his dreams, he accepted his new task in a resolute way, being well aware of his responsibility and the burden on his shoulders. But also as a bishop he wanted to live in a monastic community. He moved from the lay monastery into the bishop's house, establishing there a monastery of clerics. He lived the full common life of his brothers as much as was possible for a bishop. This monastery became very famous, for it was a nursery of learned and capable bishops for the whole North African Church. For nearly forty years Augustine was the real driving force of that Church.

The Duties of a Bishop

Primacy of the Bible

■

Bishop Augustine led a very busy life, his entire time being taken up with preaching, teaching, catechetical instruction, synods, public debates, and journeying all over North Africa. The emperor Constantine had also put the office of local judge under the care of the bishops. Every morning he had to listen to lawsuits: questions of inheritance, of guardianship, of ownership, of demarcation, and so on, a burden that he did not like at all. Moreover, as a man of study and contemplation, he was a very productive writer. His works cover some 12,000 pages in modern printing: 113 books, 247 letters, and more than 500 sermons have been preserved. How could he manage so many distinct activities? He himself more or less gives the answer when he declares that his writing was mostly done at night. Then he dictated his writings to shorthand writers.

Possidius, his friend and biographer, tells us that, after he had disposed of the care of temporal and irksome affairs, he turned his mind to meditation on the divine scriptures. The significance of the Bible in Augustine's work cannot be stressed often enough. He knew the Bible by heart; it was for him the height of all truth, the source of all teaching, and the center of all cultural and spiritual life. His theology is in the full sense of the word a biblical one. His desire was that through his voice the word of God should be heard. Another characteristic of his works is that most of what he wrote was at the request of others; only a very few books were not provoked by external circumstances. We will present here only a rough classification of his writings.

Anti-Manichean writings

■

Augustine saw it as his first duty to devote himself to the conversion of his former friends, the Manichees. What he had previously thought to be the truth, he now saw as an error. He had been responsible for the adherence to the Manichean religion of the group around him; now he tried to win back as many as possible for Christianity. Therefore, his first books aimed at refuting the Manichean doctrine.

Anti-Donatist works

■

In the following period of his life he was forced to concern himself with a very sad situation, that of a separation within the North African Church. As soon as he was ordained a priest, he had to face the disunity among Christians, caused by the schism of Donatism. Every town had a Donatist and a Catholic church, every diocese a Donatist and a

Catholic bishop, all in all over three hundred bishops on each side. The assertion that all should be one in Christ was fictitious. The Donatists pretended to be the only pure Church; they considered the Catholics as betrayers of the purity of Christian law. To understand how painful this split was, it must be remembered that the Donatists used the same holy scriptures, professed the same faith, possessed the same sacraments, and celebrated the same liturgy as did the Catholics. Hatred alone divided the Christians of Africa, and the conflict sometimes deteriorated into a civil war. With immense energy Augustine dedicated himself to restoring peace and unity, but he never completely succeeded in bringing an end to the Donatist schism - this in spite of the fact that the Conference at Carthage in 411, under the chairmanship of the very conscientious imperial delegate, Marcellinus, had decided against the Donatists. Two years later, Marcellinus himself was executed at Carthage. This murder was a heavy blow for Augustine, and it was one of the reasons why he lost his enthusiasm for the alliance between the Roman Empire and the Catholic Church.

Anti-Pelagian writings

■

In 411, after the condemnation of Donatism, Augustine must have hoped for some peace, but instead he became involved in another controversy, this time with Pelagianism. Pelagius was a servant of God, the inspirer of a more radical and ascetical Christian life, and held in high esteem by the Roman aristocrats. He insisted strongly on free will and on the efforts human beings had to make in order to reach perfection. Since perfection lies in the power of the human person, it is, according to him, something obligatory. No wonder that he was scandalized by a sentence in Augustine's *Confessions*, namely: "Command what you will; give what you command." For him this was cowardice and laxity. Pelagius' concept of Christian perfection contrasted to a certain degree with Augustine's theology and experience as a convert. Pelagius did not deny the role of God's grace, but saw it rather as a divine help coming from outside. On the other hand, like Paul, Augustine was convinced that the human will had to be strengthened from within by God's grace: all the good things we do are gifts of divine grace. It seemed to him that the Pelagian claim to be able to achieve a Church without spot or blemish continued the Donatist presumption of a pure Church. In Augustine's eyes, the human situation is much more complex. Human freedom is not a static quality. Our freedom is always in a state of becoming: human freedom is by nature a limited freedom which has to become more and more free. Augustine also believed in the doctrine of original sin, including the existence of a collective guilt, with humankind as a whole responsible for the evil in the world. Certainly one need not agree with Augustine in every detail of his view on original sin (as, for example, his conviction that unbaptized infants will be excluded from the highest form of eternal bliss). His last work, left unfinished at his death, was against the Pelagian, Julian of Eclanum, the son of an Italian bishop friend. Julian was the most able adversary Augustine ever met. Augustine's controversy with the much younger Julian was the most dramatic of his life, in which positions on both sides became more and more inflexible.

"TOO LATE HAVE I LOVED YOU,
BEAUTY SO OLD AND SO NEW;
TOO LATE HAVE I LOVED YOU.
AND SEE, YOU WERE WITHIN, AND I WAS OUTSIDE,
AND SOUGHT YOU THERE.
AND IN MY UNLOVELY STATE I PLUNGED
INTO THOSE LOVELY CREATED THINGS WHICH YOU MADE.
YOU WERE WITH ME, BUT I WAS NOT WITH YOU.
THE LOVELY THINGS KEPT ME FAR FROM YOU,
THOUGH IF THEY DID NOT HAVE THEIR EXISTENCE IN YOU,
THEY HAD NO EXISTENCE AT ALL.
YOU CALLED AND CRIED OUT LOUD
AND SHATTERED MY DEAFNESS.
YOU WERE RADIANT AND RESPLENDENT,
AND YOU PUT TO FLIGHT MY BLINDNESS.
YOU WERE FRAGRANT,
AND I DREW IN MY BREATH
AND NOW PANT AFTER YOU.
I TASTED YOU,
AND I FEEL BUT HUNGER AND THIRST FOR YOU.
YOU TOUCHED ME,
AND I AM SET ON FIRE
TO ATTAIN THE PEACE WHICH IS YOURS."

Confessions X, 27, 38

Africa in Augustine's Time

Rich and poor in North Africa

■

In order to understand the activity of Augustine as a bishop, it is necessary to know something of the situation in North Africa in his time. From of old, North Africa was the granary of the Roman Empire. It was a rich and prosperous country, thanks to its coastal plain which produced quantities of grain, and its hills further inland which produced olive oil. Oil and grain were the basis of a dynamic export trade. Whereas the power and riches of the Empire were declining visibly, North Africa resisted the crisis better than other parts of the Empire. Nonetheless in North Africa there existed great economic inequality, which caused serious social tensions. Only a minority benefited from the riches of the country and the work of the laborers. As is always the case, the weakest were the victims. All in all , however, Hippo was a prosperous city.

Decline of the Roman Empire

■

Augustine's whole life took place against the background of the decline of the Roman Empire. A sign of this was that the Roman institution of a *"defender of the rights of the poor"* had fallen into disuse at Hippo, and the African bishops asked for the reintroduction of this office without success. The decline of the standard in Italy was due to several invasions. In 410 the fortifications of Rome fell under the attack of the Visigoths of Alaric. Many Romans sought refuge in North Africa. Meditating on the sack of Rome Augustine wrote one of his most important works, twenty-two books on the city of God, in which two themes are linked together: that of the extinction of worldly civilizations and that of the eternal destiny of the human race. The prosperous situation of Africa could not remain undisturbed by the events in Italy. Newly discovered letters of Augustine give us a picture of the lamentable situation in North Africa during the last ten years of his life. Slave-hunting had become a real scourge. Criminal characters combined to attack isolated places where few people lived, to capture free citizens in order to sell them to slave-traders. Misfortune came to a climax when in 429 the Vandals and Alans under Gaiseric crossed the Strait of Gibraltar, invaded North Africa, and began their eastward advance along the coast. The destruction of Roman power in Africa had begun.

Death of Augustine

∎

In contrast to other Christian writers, Augustine did not feel hopeless in front of the political catastrophe. He had seen how the social, spiritual, and intellectual role of Christianity had grown in many parts of the world. He refused to believe that the end of the Roman Empire would mean the end of Christianity. One of his last words was a quotation from the Neoplatonic philosopher, Plotinus: "He is not truly great who thinks it of great moment that sticks and stones should crumble, and mortal things die." By his example Augustine can teach us the art of living in times of decadence. He lived in an era of revolutionary change: the old world was collapsing and a new world dawning. Europe was compelled to break out of the established framework and to seek a new future. This future was not only confined to the political sphere. It also affected the whole civilization and culture of his time: its mode of thought and its way of life.

Hippo was under siege by the Vandal troops when Augustine died on 28 August 430. He died praying the seven penitential psalms, copied and hanging before him on the wall of his room.

It will be evident that we cannot treat here all the aspects of the thought of Augustine, and that we have to make a selection among them. As the most characteristic themes, we mention the following:

1) The primacy of love.
2) Christ identifying himself with all human beings: the whole Christ.
3) Distrust of human power versus trust in divine grace.
4) Emphasis on the efficacy of God's grace in spiritual life.
5) Love for the Word of God and emphasis on the value of scriptural reading.

The Primacy of Love

Love and true happiness

■

Augustine's writings begin with the question as to how a human being can find true happiness. There is no human being who does not desire to be happy. Desire has to do with love, for nobody desires what he does not love. Love consists in the will to become one with the object which is loved. But not every object of longing and love can make a person happy. Only an everlasting and imperishable good can make us truly happy, for only such a good excludes all fear of loss of the object which is loved. God alone can guarantee such a happiness. Love unites us with God as our eternal, everlasting good, and thus makes us participate in God's eternity. This happens according to the principle that a human being becomes what he loves: "Let him love the earth, he will become earth; let him love the eternal God, he will share in God's eternity."

Love: the whole message of the Bible

■

According to Augustine the whole message of the Bible can be reduced to the two commandments, love of God and love of one's neighbor. He writes: "My hope in the name of Christ is not sterile, because not only do I believe, my God, that on the two love commandments depend the whole law and the prophets, but I have also experienced, and I still experience every day, that not a single mystery or obscure word of holy scripture becomes clear for me, unless I meet with these two commandments." Augustine remains faithful here to the Pauline line of thought: Love is the fulfilling of the law (Rom 13:10) and: Love is the end of the command (1 Tm 1:5). The word "end" does not mean that love puts an end to all other precepts or abolishes them, but love is the perfection to which every precept should be referred. These two love commandments are not only characteristic of the new but also of the old law. Consequently, Christ's words *I give you a new commandment: love one another just as I have loved you* (Jn 13:34) did not only renew the apostles and ourselves, but also all the patriarchs, prophets, and righteous who lived at the time of the first covenant.

Loving with God's love

∎

God is love. Revealing himself as good and merciful, God reveals himself as love. This becomes for us an appeal, a demand, and a command to love human beings as God loves them. The highest form of love of our brothers and sisters consists in loving them with God's love given to us by the Holy Spirit. Thus our love is a participation in the love of God which encompasses every human being, even our enemies. Our love has to mirror God's love. When Augustine speaks of love, he means love as a divine gift, which endows the human will with a new desire, a striving for the divine truth, wisdom, peace, and justice. To love with this love excludes all that is sinful, namely possessive or egotistic greed: pride, pretension, self-praise, or honor, and seeking only one's own profit. The fact that love is a gift of God

applies in the first place to love for God, for he alone can give himself to us. He has loved us first. But the same principle applies to love for one's neighbor. The Holy Spirit in us also enflames us to love the human being alongside us. According to Augustine, a merely natural love for one another is not enough, because then we easily neglect God as our supreme good. To love the other as ourselves means that he or she may find his or her good where we ourselves find it, namely in God. Only in this light can we rightly understand Augustine's famous sentence, "Love, and then do what you want, for from that root nothing but good can spring." Love is the most difficult law we have; it never means that we are free to do as we like.

67

Temporary primacy of love of one's neighbor

■

Seen in the light of the foregoing considerations, Augustine defends even a temporary primacy of the love of one's neighbor. Temporary means: here on earth, as long as we have to care for our fellow human beings. It is true that love of God comes first as a commandment, but equally true that love of one's neighbor comes first on the level of practice. In order to love God we have to begin with love of our neighbor: "These commandments must always be reflected upon, they must be pondered, they must be adhered to, they must be acted upon, they must be fulfilled. The love of God is first in the order of commandment, but the love of one's neighbor is first in the order of action. In loving your neighbor, and in being concerned about him or her, you get going. Where could you go, except to the Lord God?" The reason why this is so is the fact that both loves include one another and cannot be separated. Therefore, it is sufficient to mention just one of them. Appealing to the authority of Paul and John, Augustine draws the conclusion that it is not without reason that holy scripture commonly puts one commandment for both. The reason for this appears clearly from the following text: "Why does Paul in both Galatians and Romans mention only love of one's neighbor? Is not the reason that, since love of God is not so frequently put to the test, people can deceive themselves about it? In love for one's neighbor, however, they can be more easily convinced that they do not love God, when they act unjustly toward other people. By the precept of love for one's neighbor they are made aware of their shortcomings. Some of the Galatians were deceiving themselves that they loved God. They were shown clearly that they did not because of the hatred among brothers and sisters." Thus the love of one's neighbor is the concrete norm for our love of God, for by its practical nature it excludes any self-deception. Love of our neighbor is the most concrete means of giving expression to our love of God.

Diuina tandem de SS.^{ma} Trinitate volumina, aliosq3 innumeros eruditus scriba ex omnigenæ sapientiæ suæ thesauro protulit libros, tractatus, sermones, epistolas &c. Possid. in vita et indiculo.

The Whole Christ

Together one body

■

"If the only word in scripture were that one word of the Holy Spirit that God is love, it would be amply sufficient and we would not need to seek further." According to Augustine, the chief reason for the incarnation was God's love, for he gave his Son to us. Thus the Son became the incarnation of God's love. If God is love, it follows that God does not wish to remain aloof without any relationship with the human world. Love requires companionship. God the Father begot an only Son, but God did not want the only Son to remain alone; God gave him all human beings as brothers and sisters. Christ stands in an all-embracing relationship with the whole of humanity, because his love extends to every human being without exception. In love we discover a double movement: a longing to become one with the beloved, and the need to maintain a certain distance out of respect for the personal identity of the person we love. Love results in a reciprocal presence without destruction of the other: a friend in his or her friend, a husband in his wife, a mother in her child. Christ too identified himself with every human being, and is present in them. Augustine calls this union: the whole Christ. He bases his insight on Paul's doctrine of the relationship between Christ as the head and us as the body: *Just as the body is one and has many members, and all the members, many as they are, are together one body, so also the Christ* (1 Cor 12:12). The one Christ encompasses the head as well as the limbs, and this union is as intimate as that which reigns in a living body. Thus Christ participates in our life, and we participate in the life of Christ.

Honor God in one another (Rule)

■

Since God is the center of Christ's life, many of the above-mentioned ideas also apply to God. The way to be one with every human being is to feel at one with him or her in a higher unity: in the concern of God for all. Each human being is a place where God is. Each one belongs to God who loves them all. If we too love them all, we honor God. Only when people become one another's sisters and brothers are they the new temple of God, that is, the place of his presence, for God dwells nowhere but in love. Before speaking of a church as the house of God, we should consider ourselves: "This church building is the house of our prayers, but we ourselves are the real house of God. Together we form the house of the Lord only if we are joined to one another in love." Thus love of God and love of one's neighbor are competing acts, but they embrace each other in one great dynamic movement.

Christix in the poor

■

Augustine finds inspiration principally in two biblical texts: *Lord, when did we see you hungry and feed you, or thirsty and gave you to drink? And the king will answer: "Amen, I tell you, anything you did for one of the least of mine, you did for me"* (Mt 25:37-40) and: *"Saul, Saul, why do you persecute me?"* (Acts 9:4). As regards this last text, Augustine remarks that the risen Christ does not say: Why do you persecute my disciples? but: Why are you persecuting me? Such an identification of Christ with the poor, the outcasts, and the persecuted meant for Augustine the recognition of their human dignity. "Be faithful to Christ in his poverty" is the same as saying "Be faithful to your neighbor in his poverty." Matthew 25 shows Augustine how Christ is still present in this world and how he is to be comprehended by the faithful. The suffering and poverty of Jesus Christ is continually reflected in the life and history of suffering and oppressed human beings. Here in this pilgrimage on earth, the hungry Christ is fed, the thirsty Christ is given to drink, the naked Christ is clothed, he is welcomed in the person of the stranger and visited in the sick. When human beings are in want, it is Christ who is in want: "Go onto the road. Christ the stranger is not absent. Do you think that you are not permitted to welcome Christ? How can this be? you ask. Listen: *What you did to one of the least of mine, you did to me.* He who is rich is in need until the end of time. He is truly in need, not in his head, but in his members."

Option for the poor

■

"We are the servants of his Church, and most of all of its weakest members, whatever sort of members we ourselves may be in this same body." This statement of Augustine shows clearly his deep concern for the poor and powerless. From certain, newly discovered letters we know a lot about his social activities. There we see him asking the emperor to promulgate a new law against the slave-traders. We see him very worried about the sale of children, which the Christian emperors had allowed for a period of twenty-five years in order to prevent child-murder when parents were not able to feed their newborn babies. The tenant farmers, especially, had to resort to the desperate measure of hiring out or selling their children. This often led to perpetual slavery which was not permitted by the law, and Augustine protested vehemently against this abuse of children. He had the lot of children very much at heart, for he saw it as his task as bishop to protect orphans so that they would not be robbed of everything by strangers. He also considered it his duty to care for abandoned children. With regard to the poor, it was the custom of the Church of Hippo to give help to every person, whoever he or she was: a non-Christian, a prostitute, or a fighter in the arena. Augustine did not agree with the text: *Be merciful, but do not help the sinner* (Sir 12:4-7). He comments: "Let us treat them with human decency because they are human beings. Take pity on the condition that is common to all."

72

Friendship and Common Life

Mutual love

■

Augustine was very social-minded and friendly. He never wanted to be alone, and he hardly ever spent a moment of his life without friends, or blood-relatives, close by him. No thinker in the early Church was so preoccupied with the nature of human relationships. Even in his youth, he formed a core of abiding friendships. He describes them in a beautiful passage of his *Confessions:* "All kinds of things rejoiced my soul in their company: to talk and laugh, and to do each other kindnesses; to read pleasant books to gether; to pass from lightest jesting to talk of the deepest things; to disagree without rancor, as one might disagree with oneself, and then to reason through this very rare dissension our normal agreement; to teach each other and to learn from each other; to be impatient for the return of the absent, and to welcome them with joy on their homecoming. These, and such-like things, proceeding from our hearts as we gave affection and received it back, and shown by face, by voice, by the eyes, and by a thousand other pleasing gestures, kindled a flame which fused our souls together, and, of many, made us one." This is what he loved in his friends. He felt guilty if he did not love the person who loved him and if that love was not returned. To give love and to receive love, in short, mutual love, this is Augustine's definition of friendship. The measure of true friendship is not temporal advantage, but unselfish love, based on a similarity of character, ideas, interest, and commitment.

Limitations of human friendship

■

Human nature possesses two great natural goods: marriage and friendship. In another text Augustine declares that two things are essential for the human being, namely life and friendship, and both are nature's gifts. God created the human being that he or she might exist and live. But if a human person is not to remain solitary, there must be friendship. He who tries to forbid all friendly conversation must be aware that he breaks the ties of all human relationships. Faithfulness, trust, veracity, and stability are the most significant qualities of friendship. Augustine considered, however, all human things perishable, a realization that came upon him most powerfully when one of his young friends died. The experience of the loss of this friend did not drive him into a denial of friendship, but showed him that friendship has to be based on love of God, for "he alone does not lose a beloved one, for all are beloved in God, who is not lost." But not only death can snatch a friend from our midst; human weakness and instability can also cause friendship to change into treachery, baseness, and even hatred. Therefore, Augustine seeks the basis of faithfulness and stability among friends in God and in Christ. He had become aware of the fact that Cicero's definition of friendship, "Friendship is an agreement on all human and divine things, with benevolence and love," also encompassed the domain of the divine.

Friendship in religious life

■

In contrast to many founders of religious communities, Augustine gave friendship an important place in the common life of the religious. He taught his young monks that they were not obliged to accept immediately everyone in friendship, but that it should be their wish to accept everyone as a friend. Their attitude toward others should be such that the possibility of taking them into their friendship remains open. Although we never will succeed in penetrating fully another's innermost self, he called our attention to the fact that "Nobody can truly be known, except through friendship." And when his monks asked him when they could call another a friend, he answered: "We can consider another person as a friend, if we dare to entrust to him or her all our innermost thoughts." He also saw friendship as a help and consolation for himself, describing his monastic experience as follows: "I admit that I readily throw myself entirely on the love of my most intimate friends, especially when I am wearied with the world's scandals, and I find rest in that love, free of anxiety. This is because I feel that God, upon whom I cast myself without fear, and in whom I find secure rest, is present there. In this security of mine, I do not fear the uncertainty of tomorrow and of human weakness. What ideas and thoughts I entrust to a human being who is full of Christian charity, and has become for me a faithful friend, I do not entrust to a human being, but to God, in whom this person abides, and who made him or her a faithful friend."

Influence

■

In Western Europe, particularly in England and Northern France, Augustine's ideas on friendship had a strong influence on medieval Cluniac-Cistercian religious life, especially on Peter the Venerable, Bernard of Clairvaux, Aelred of Rievaulx, and Peter of Celle. It was only during the fifteenth century, apparently, that there came a flight from friendship because of the conviction that friendship among religious would undermine the integrity of life in religious community.

The *Rule* of Augustine

Rule for a lay community
■

Augustine is best known as a restless searcher for truth, as a convert, bishop, and theologian. He is less well known as a monk. However, we can only understand his personality fully if we keep in mind that his sole wish after his conversion was to be a servant of God or, in a word, a monk. As a priest and even as a bishop he lived a monastic life. But what is more: in writing the oldest, still existing, monastic Rule of the West, he exerted an unusually great influence on the Christian ideal of religious life. He wrote his *Rule* about 397. By that time he had already had a certain experience of religious life. His first foundation took place at Thagaste in 388. In 391, as a priest, he founded a monastery for lay monks at Hippo. When he was ordained bishop, he set up a monastery for clerics in his bishop's house at Hippo in 395/396. It was there that he wrote his *Rule* which is clearly intended for the lay community he had to leave when he became bishop.

One soul and one heart
■

His *Rule* is a set of condensed, inspiring principles, a summary of the oral teaching he had given to his former companions who were now deprived of his presence. The purpose of the precepts given in the *Rule* is to create a common life based on love and harmony among the members of the monastery. Augustine's ideal was the first Christian community of Jerusalem, as described in the Acts of the Apostles 4:32: *The whole group of believers was of one soul and one heart. No one claimed any of his possessions as his own, but everything was held in common.* Augustine considered the revival of this ideal important for his time, and he saw in it a major contribution toward the promotion of the reign of God in this world.

The structure of the *Rule* shows clearly Augustine's primary concern: the building up of a real and loving common life, the cultivation of good interpersonal relationships. This unity, however, should be centered upon God, for unanimity as such does not in itself make a group a religious community. Its religious character depends on the fact that the members move toward God together. Such a life encompasses the whole of concrete human existence: sharing in one another's faith, hope, affections, ideals, feelings, thoughts, activities, responsibilities, shortcomings, failures, and sins. This basic ideal is set out in chapter I: united, soul and heart, striving for God, and expressed in a sharing of material and spiritual goods, and in humility as a necessary condition for love.

Practical applications

∎

The other short chapters 2-8 of the *Rule* are simply practical elaborations of the fundamental first chapter: common prayer, community and care for the body, mutual responsibility in good and evil, rendering services to one another, love and conflict, love in authority and obedience, love of spiritual beauty and true freedom. One is immediately struck by the fact that very few concrete rules are given. Nowhere is it a question of details, but always of the essence of things and of the human heart. Thus, the way of interiority is repeatedly applied in the *Rule*: the external must be a sign of what is occurring inwardly. The external ought not to remain empty, but should be animated from within. The transition from exterior to interior occurs in the *Rule* no less than seven times: from verbal prayer to prayer of the heart, from physical hunger to hunger for the word of God, from not pleasing by clothes to pleasing by our inner way of life, from seeing to desiring a sexual partner, from a physical wound to a wound in the heart, from appearances to the inner clothing of the heart, from forgiving with words to true forgiveness from the heart. A final characteristic of Augustine's *Rule* is the almost total absence of emphasis on asceticism; that is, leading an ascetical life in a material sense by denying oneself food and drink, or by self-chastisement. The accent is rather on living in community as a victory over self-seeking.

A call to evangelical equality

∎

We can characterize the *Rule* of Augustine as a call to evangelical equality of all people. It voices the Christian demand to bring all men and women into full community. At the same time it sounds a protest against the inequality in a society which is so clearly marked by possessiveness, pride, and power. According to Augustine, therefore, a monastic community should offer an alternative by striving to build up a community that is motivated by love and friendship. In this sense the *Rule* is also critical of society.

Contemplation and Action

Three types of life

■

In his book *The City of God*, Augustine discusses three types of life: the contemplative, the active, and one which is a mixture of both. He clearly prefers this last mixed form, that is, contemplation combined with a public function. No one ought to be so completely absorbed by contemplation as not to think of one's neighbor's advantage, nor so active as to neglect the contemplation of divine truth. Contemplation is not merely an intellectual activity, for it consists in loving and searching for God, in such a way that the searcher does not withhold from his or her brothers and sisters the fruit of his or her contemplation. In this way, contemplative monastic life too has its own responsibility; one should share the truth that one has discovered and not keep it for oneself. Thus the pure monastic life is not to be regarded as an existence deprived of activity.

Active life: a greater danger

■

The unselfish character of religious life ought to be present still more explicitly in the active life which must never be a form of self-seeking, but has to contribute to the well-being of others. In the text of *The City of God*, Augustine described in

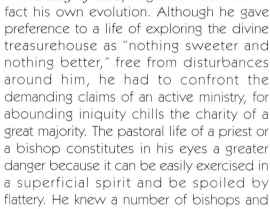

fact his own evolution. Although he gave preference to a life of exploring the divine treasurehouse as "nothing sweeter and nothing better," free from disturbances around him, he had to confront the demanding claims of an active ministry, for abounding iniquity chills the charity of a great majority. The pastoral life of a priest or a bishop constitutes in his eyes a greater danger because it can be easily exercised in a superficial spirit and be spoiled by flattery. He knew a number of bishops and had often judged them severely, considering himself a more learned and better man. Since he looked upon priesthood as an office that is public and social, he saw himself faced with the question of how to put his own faith at the service of others for their salvation, without looking for any personal profit, but only for the advantage of the great multitude. He did not want, he said, to be a bishop who sat on his throne like a scarecrow which fulfilled its task by standing immobile in a field.

Christian and minister

■

Augustine, therefore, makes a distinction between being a Christian and having a pastoral ministry. The fact of being a Christian is bestowed on him for his own benefit, but that of being a minister is given for the interests of others, so that there is no absolute gap between clergy and believers. The first task of both is to be good Christians. Augustine frequently tells his people: we too are sheep along with you; I am your fellow servant, your fellow worker in the Lord's vineyard, your fellow disciple in the same school of Christ. And in one of his sermons he states openly: "What do I want? What do I wish? What do I desire? Why do I speak? Why do I sit here? Why do I live? Only with this intention, that together we may live with Christ. That is my desire, my honor, my joy, and my wealth. But I don't want to be saved without you." Ministry is not a question of honor or power, but of service. The expression "servant of the servants of Christ" stems from Augustine, and was later taken over by the popes. His favorite term to describe this serving task is always "burden," the burden which soldiers had to carry on their backs. The apostolate is a service of teaching rather than of commanding, of exhorting rather than of threatening. It is striking that Augustine always describes the task of a priest or bishop in the following way: he is a minister of word and sacrament. This order cannot be explained as a mere accident, for he considered the proclaiming of the word of God a more difficult task than administering the sacraments.

Mary and Martha

■

However important pastoral work, undertaken out of love for God and neighbor, may be, it cannot be fulfilled without a life of contemplation, prayer, and study. A good pastor has to be a good hearer of God's word before he can speak it. He has to live as he speaks, and to speak as he hears. Listening to the divine word is an aspect of contemplation. On the heights of the mountain, like the apostle Peter, the pastoral worker will receive the light and spiritual food he has to distribute to others. The graceful and beautiful Rachel is for Augustine the image of contemplative life, and the dull-eyed, but fertile, Leah the image of the laboring preacher. The same could be said of Mary and Martha, but Augustine refuses to interpret Jesus' words to Martha: *"Martha, Martha, you worry and fret about so many things. It is Mary who has chosen the better part"* as a reproach: "How could Jesus address a reproach to Martha who rejoiced at receiving such a sublime guest? If it were a reproach, there would be no one anymore to care for the needy. Everybody would choose the better part and say: let us spend all our time listening to the word of God. But if this were to happen, nobody would be there to care for the stranger in the city, for the person who needs bread or clothes, nobody to visit the sick, nobody to liberate prisoners, nobody to bury the dead. Works of mercy done to those in need are necessary here on earth."

81

Augustine's *Rule* in the World

The night of time

■

One cannot call Augustine the founder of a religious order in the modern, juridical sense of the word. We know for certain that he founded at least three monasteries, and desired that monastic life should spread all over Africa. From Possidius' *Life of Augustine* we also know that there was a convent at Hippo, under the direction of Augustine's sister. Moreover, a number of monks from Augustine's monasteries became bishops in other African towns, where they founded monastic communities after the model they had known at Hippo. Thus the North African Church had some fifteen monasteries with a marked Augustinian character. Even after the Vandal invasions and the death of Augustine monasticism persisted in Africa. Its extinction only came with the Arab invasions during the years 647-668. In the period between 430 and 668, many monks went into exile. They fled to nearby countries, but we do not know whether they continued to live in communities following the *Rule* of Augustine. Of the dispersed monks of Africa, we can say that they walked into the night of time. There is no certainty at all about an historical continuity between the monasteries of Augustine and later monastic life outside Africa.

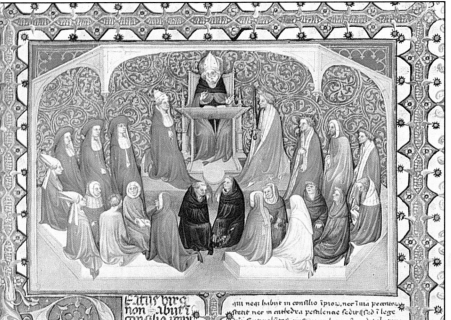

Influence of the *Rule*

■

If we follow the history of the manuscripts of the *Rule* of Augustine, we get a rather different picture. We see then that the spirit of this *Rule* indeed survived during the subsequent centuries. No less than fourteen manuscripts, dating from before the year 1000, have come down to us. From the time of Caesarius of Arles (+ 542/543), via Benedict of Nursia (+ 550), till the time of Benedict of Aniane (+ 820/821), we notice the influence of Augustine's *Rule*. But we have to wait till the end of the ninth century to find an intense longing for a full common life according to the spirituality of Augustine among the Canons Regular at Reims (975). This reform movement led in the last decades of the eleventh century to the acceptance of the *Rule* of Augustine by the Canons Regular as the norm for their common life. In the twelfth century, they were followed by the Victorines, Canons Regular of the abbey dedicated to Saint Victor founded in 1108 at Paris, by Norbert of Xanten who founded the Premonstratensian Canons in 1120, and by Dominic for the Order of the Friars Preachers in 1215. Furthermore, the *Rule* of Augustine was adopted by the Crutched Friars (O.S.C.) founded probably by Dietrich von Zell around 1210, by the Mercedarians founded by Peter Nolasco in 1218, by the Canonesses of the Holy Sepulcher founded at the beginning of the thirteenth century, and by the Order of the Servites of the Holy Virgin Mary founded in 1240. In 1244 the Holy See united several

groups of Hermits under the name Order of the Hermits of Saint Augustine (O.E.S.A.), now known as the Order of Saint Augustine (O.S.A.). In the following centuries we find a considerable number of communities living under the *Rule* of Augustine, of which the most important are: the Brethren of the Common Life, Augustinian Canons and representatives of the *Devotio Moderna* together with the famous monastery of Windesheim, founded by Florentius Radewijns respectively in 1384 and 1387; the Alexians, of whom most adopted the *Rule* in 1450; the Brothers Hospitallers founded by John of God around 1540; the Piarists founded by Joseph Calasanctius in 1597; the Visitation Order of Holy Mary founded by Jane de Chantal and Francis de Sales in 1610; the Sisters of Our Lady of Charity (of the Refuge) and its branches, founded by John Eudes in 1641; the Barmherzige Brüder von Maria Hilf founded by Peter Friedhofen in 1850; the Augustinians of the Assumption founded at Nimes by Emmanuel d'Alzon in 1850.

History of the Order of Saint Augustine

From Hermits to Mendicant Friars

■

In the tenth and eleventh centuries, all over Europe and particularly in Italy, there were many monks who had settled in remote places, the so-called hermitages. One of the most famous hermitages is that of Lecceto near Siena. The origin of these little congregations must be sought in the desire for a deeper spiritual way of life as a protest against an easy and poor evangelical lifestyle. But in the thirteenth century the eremitical life no longer corresponded to the needs of the surrounding world, which required a new style of religious life. The world and social life had changed notably with the growth of commerce, the rise of capitalism, the development of the cities, the origin of the bourgeoisie as a social power, and the foundation of universities. Monastic theology had become scholastic theology. Whereas the intellectual education had been for centuries the patrimony of the clergy, it then also passed into the hands of lay people. In this climate movements of voluntary poverty came into existence, which adopted a critical attitude toward the worldly life of the Church. This attitude was at the root of the creation of the mendicant orders: Franciscans, Dominicans, Carmelites, and Augustinians. The Church needed them in order to stem the tide of the new mentality. This was the reason why several contemplative congregations of hermits, some of which lived under the *Rule* of Augustine, wanted to become united as a juridical entity, the Order of Saint Augustine. The union of March 1244 was soon followed by the Great Union in 1256, which was approved by Pope Alexander IV. From that moment on they tended to concentrate their work in the towns.

Evolution through the ages

As is the case for every medieval religious order, one can clearly distinguish five periods.

1. 1244-1350: PERIOD OF MATURATION AND PROGRESSION

After the Great Union of 1256, and even here and there before this date, the Order expanded rapidly from Italy into France, England, Germany, and Spain.

From these centers, it spread all over Europe: from Hungary and Poland to Portugal, from Ireland to the Aegean Sea, Crete, Corfu, Cyprus, and Rhodes, with a few settlements in the Balkans, the Ukraine, and the Baltic countries. From 1264 on, we also find contemplative Augustinian nuns. Already in 1293, the Augustinians had moved into the monastery situated on what is now called the Quai des Grands Augustins in Paris, which became an important center of studies. There were twenty-four provinces in 1329. The expansion continued till 1350, although here and there one already discovers some signs of slackening.

2. 1350-1538: DECADENCE AND OBSERVANT MOVEMENTS

A period of enthusiasm is normally followed by a period of regression. Zeal for the evangelical life as well as for the common life had faded. There were several reasons for this, such as the poor condition of theological education, the slackening of ecclesiastical authority, and the gap between the higher and the lower clergy. The late Middle Ages saw the rise of local reformed congregations as a reaction against spiritual laxity. We can see that many were filled with nostalgia for the old eremitical life-style. Such reforms were often accompanied by serious tensions between "observants," the advocates of renewal, and "conventuals," the advocates of the old customs. One of these reformed congregations was the congregation of Saxony (1438), to which Martin Luther, the founder of the great German Reformation, belonged. The Order suffered considerably from the effects of the Reformation. Augustinian monasteries in Germany, Belgium, and the Netherlands were strongly influenced by the Saxon reform movement. Several monks chose Luther's side. Already in 1523 at Brussels, two Belgian Augustinians, adherents of the Lutheran doctrine, had died at the stake. It is also true, however, that the Calvinists did the same at Ghent with Augustinians who did not renounce their faith. Apart from the Reformation, another serious reason for the declining number of Augustinians was pestilence and famine all over Europe. Between 1348 and 1351 no less than 5,084 members of the Order died from the Black Death.

Rita of Cascia

■

We do not possess much historically reliable information about Rita. The earliest information stems from the inscription and the paintings on the coffin that contained her body. Born in the last decades of the fourteenth century, she married young - according to oral tradition - and had two children. She was widowed around the age of twenty-five when her husband was murdered. This killing was probably in connection with the fighting between the towns and the castles, in other words between the Guelphs and the Ghibellines. After the death of her husband, she entered into the monastery of Saint Mary Magdalene in Cascia. During the last years of her life she shared in the sufferings of Christ's passion through a thorn wound that the Lord granted her. Because she was against all the violence caused by the social conflicts in the region of Cascia, she was considered a peacemaker and was given the title "advocate of the impossible." She died in 1457 and was canonized by Leo XIII in 1900.

John of Sahagún

■

John was born about 1430, and studied at the Benedictine abbey of Sahagún in León province. He assisted the bishop of Burgos, Alonso of Cartagena, who ordained him to the priesthood in about 1454. When Bishop Alonso died in 1456, John renounced his chaplaincy and the canonry he had in Burgos, and was transferred to Salamanca. From 1457 till 1461 he studied canon law and theology there. In 1460 he was named preacher of the city, a priest in the church of Saint Stephen, and a member of the university college of Saint Bartholomew. But in 1463 he gave up, and took the Augustinian habit. He was twice prior of the community of Salamanca the principal house of his observant congregation, reformed by John of Alarcon in 1438. He died there in 1479. His biographer was convinced that he was murdered by one of the men whose vices he had denounced, for John, the apostle of Salamanca, had much boldness in his preaching, always saying the truth. He was canonized in 1690.

John Stone

■

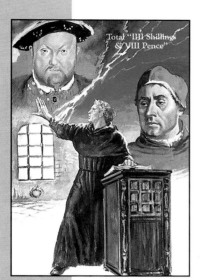

Between the years 1535 and 1692 several hundred English Catholics were put to death. A group of forty, among them John Stone, were canonized in 1970. John was a member of the English Augustinian Province. He probably began his religious life at Canterbury, where the Order had had a foundation since 1318. In 1538, the Dominican Richard Ingworth, bishop of Dover, a creature of Cromwell, presented the deed of surrender and letter of submission to the prior and his community at Canterbury. John Stone refused to recognize the king as supreme head of the Church. Ingworth isolated John from the rest of the community in the hope of persuading him to sign. John persisted in his refusal, and Cromwell detained John for a year in prison. In 1539 John was executed at Canterbury: first he was hanged, then the executioner cut out his heart, his head and limbs were severed from his body and boiled in oil; later they were placed on the city gates as a warning to others. In the same year 1539 the Order ceased to exist in England; not a single house remained.

Thomas of Villanova

■

Thomas was born in 1486 at Fuenllana, Spain. Later he became professor of philosophy at the University of Alcalá de Henares. Thomas refused an invitation to become professor at the University of Salamanca, and preferred to enter the Order in 1516. He had a great influence on the progress of study and spirituality therein, through his teaching and preaching. While he was prior in Valladolid, Charles V presented him in 1544 as a candidate for the archbishopric of Valencia. In his writings we find a synthesis between the thought of Augustine and the doctrine of Thomas Aquinas, between mysticism and scholasticism. He was a defender of the true mystics and this became the reason why some of his writings were placed on the Index in 1599. He was also a promoter of the *Devotio moderna* in Spain. His concern for the little ones, the sick, the young in danger, and the poor were the main characteristics of his apostolate, so that people called him "the father of the poor." In this respect, he repeated Augustine's words: "The superfluous goods of the rich do by right belong to the poor. It is Jesus who in the poor receives our gifts." As a contemporary of Luther, in his sermons he vehemently accused the clergy and the monks of moral deterioration and unfaithfulness to the gospel. He was canonized in 1658.

The Japanese martyrs

■

Just when there were high hopes for a favorable future in the Japanese missions, the situation worsened greatly with the arrival of the English and Dutch who informed the emperor of Japan that he did not need to accept Spanish missionaries to maintain business relations with the countries of Europe. In 1614 a decree of expulsion for all missionaries and the destruction of their churches was published. The Augustinian Fernando de Ayala was put to death by the sword in 1617, followed some months later by a Japanese Christian, Andrew Yoshida, from Nagasaki. The Augustinian Pedro de Zúñiga fell into the hands of the Dutch and English who handed him over to the persecutors. In 1622 he was burned alive, and with him Captain Joaquin Hiroyama, who had taken him on his ship. Bartolomé Gutiérrez had escaped the persecution since 1618, spending the daytime hidden in a cave and the nights with his flock. In 1629 he was captured together with his catechist, John Shozaburo, and burned to death in 1632. In 1634 the Portuguese Augustinian, Francisco Correira, was murdered at Nagasaki. The first native Augustinians, Thomas Jihioye and Miguel de San José, could hide themselves more easily than their foreign brothers, but were nevertheless killed in 1637. According to some sources, more than six hundred Augustinian tertiaries have suffered a martyr's death. One of them, a girl only twenty-three years old, Magdalena of Nagasaki, was canonized in 1987.

THE SAINTS

*Thérèse
of
Lisieux*

"The greatest Saint of modern times"

When Pope Pius X (1903-1914) described Sister Thérèse of the Child Jesus (who died in 1897) as "the greatest saint of modern times", in a private audience with a missionary, his words were prophetic. He himself was canonised in 1954.

As the centenary of the "Entry into Life" of this young Carmelite nun, who died unknown in a provincial monastery, approaches, we can see how right he was. Is there any saint - apart, perhaps, from Saint Francis of Assisi, who is better known and loved in the world than this young girl who was canonised in 1925, made Patron Saint of the Universal Missions in 1927, Second Patron Saint of France, with her "beloved sister", Joan of Arc, in 1944 - and who has been made a Doctor of the Church.

There is hardly a church without her statue (tasteless though some of them may be). Her picture has been sold in millions throughout the world and, since 1961, 47 authentic photographs have revealed her true face, which is totally unlike the picture postcard portrayals giving her the insipid delicacy of a juvenile film star.

To English speakers, Thérèse is the "Little Flower", to the Spanish speakers, "Teresita", to the Portuguese "Teresinha", to the Muslims in Cairo Saint Fatma.

Her thoughts, set down on her superiors' instructions and published as "Story of a Soul" in 1898, are a world-bestseller and have been translated into countless languages (more than 60 languages and dialects). Successive teams took forty years to prepare the critical edition of the original texts. On 18 February 1993, Pope John Paul II was presented with the eight volumes of the "Complete Works", on which all future research will be based.

Thousands of books and articles have already been written about Thérèse in all the world's languages. Theologians, religious writers, novelists and psychologists have thoroughly analyzed her personality and message. From Father Philipon to Cardinal Urs von Balthasar, from Fathers Congar, Boyer, Durrwell, Bro and Laurentin to Cardinals Journet, Daniélou and Poupard, theological studies abound. And all the popes of this century, from Leo XIII to John Paul II, have paid tribute to her spirituality.

Basilica.

Pius XII called her "the greatest healer of modern times". In fact between 1910 and 1925, the Lisieux Carmel published seven volumes of the "Shower of Roses" (3750 pages), detailing amazing cures, apparitions and conversions, described by people throughout the world who experienced them. This is only the tip of the iceberg. Many of those who owe Thérèse so much have never actually told anyone how she touched their lives. This bears out the mysterious words she spoke on 17 July 1897, while she was dying of tuberculosis in the Infirmary: "I shall spend my heaven doing good on earth". She added: "I feel that my work is just beginning, my work of making people love God as I love Him, of giving my "Little Way" to other souls".

Another important fact: her special message, that "Way of Spiritual Childhood", which she discovered around the age of 22, when she turned into a spiritual leader who has guided millions throughout the world, inspired thousands of religious vocations and paved the way for the Second Vatican Council (Vatican II): a return to the Word of God, Christology, Ecclesiology, Mariology and so on... In her quiet, unobtrusive way, she brought about a spiritual revolution, which marked the transition from a Jansenist form of religion marked by fear of a God seen mainly as a God of Vengeance to a daring confidence in God as the essential source of Love, Life and Joy.

In 1937, a pamphleteering psychiatrist claimed that the "Glorious Hurricane" (Pius XI) unleashed by Thérèse was an infallible sign that the Catholic Church was in its death throes. The universal exaltation of an insignificant "neurotic" was proof that a masochistic religion was on the way out at last. Fifty years on, today's psychologists and religious writers know a great deal more about Thérèse Martin and her world, and are quick to acknowledge the wonders wrought by grace in the mind and heart of a child stricken by the loss of her mother when she herself was only four and a half years old. Indeed, Thérèse's path to sainthood is a source of comfort and inspiration to countless victims of emotional or other crises today. Sainthood is not reserved for "normal" people (who are these "normal" people anyway?).

The "Little Way" is not some sleight of hand for getting to heaven on the cheap. It is the modern realisation of the Gospel injunction: "Except ye be converted, and become as little children, ye shall not enter into the Kingdom of heaven" (Mt 18, 3).

On 2 June 1980, Pope John Paul II, the first Pope to make the pilgrimage to Lisieux, put it strongly: "The 'Little Way' is the way of 'Holy Childhood'. It is a way which both confirms and renews the most **fundamental** and **universal** truth. After all, which of the Gospel's truths is more fundamental and more universal than this: God is our Father and we are His children?".

In 1897, 18 600 people lived in Lisieux. Today, there are a bare 24,500, but this small town in Normandy has now become an international crossroad. From all over the world, pilgrims flock to the town where Thérèse lived. Despite the pessimists, a basilica was built with the help of worldwide donations between 1929 and 1937, at the very heart of the economic crisis. Today, even this is too small, and an international visitors' centre will be needed for the centenary in 1997... and afterwards. For this is only the beginning! As early as 1932, one of Thérèse's most ardent admirers, the Carmelite Father Marie Eugène of the Child Jesus declared: "She, a little child, will teach the souls who will make up the army of the last days to give themselves over entirely to God's mercy. We are at the start of her mission. The great works are still to come, and they will show her at last for what she really is: great among all the saints!"

Time will tell... But there are many signs that a demoralised society is turning again to the Gospels, and that faith, hope and love are being renewed among the directionless young - signs which show that the life and message of a young girl who "died for love" of God and humanity will always bear fruit. For she has promised to work for us here on earth, "to the end of time". This is plain enough. God always finishes what He begins.

Guy Gaucher
Auxiliary Bishop of Bayeux and Lisieux.

© OCL Lisieux

Alençon.

Les Buissonnets.

Story of a life

Childhood in Alençon (1873-1877)

Of farming and army stock, the Martin family had solid roots in Normandy and Mayenne. Brought up in a series of military camps, Louis Martin (1823-1894) thought seriously of entering a monastery. But this was not to be, and he turned to clock- and watchmaking instead. Zélie Guérin (1831-1877) was also unsuccessful in her attempt to enter the religious order of the sisters of the Hôtel-Dieu. She learned the Alençon lace-making technique and soon mastered this painstaking craft. They married in 1858 and had nine children. Four, including two boys, died in infancy.

Thérèse, the youngest, was born on 2 January 1873. She was put out to nurse for a year and became a lively, mischievous and self-confident child; she thrived on the love which surrounded her in this Christian household, where prayer, the liturgy and practical good works formed the basis of her own ardent love of Jesus - her desire to please him and the Virgin Mary. But disaster struck suddenly, when her mother died of breast cancer in the summer of 1877.

Lisieux - Les Buissonnets

Her father was left to raise the five girls, ranging from four to seventeen. His brother-in-law, Isidore Guérin, a chemist in Lisieux, invited them all to come and live with him in this small town, with its population of just 18 600 people. They moved on 15 November 1877.

Thérèse spent eleven years at Les Buissonnets, a fine house with a quiet garden, some way from the centre of the town. Her sisters, Marie and Pauline, took care of her education. "Poor Léonie" was a difficult child. Céline, nearly four years older, was her favourite playmate. Louis Martin was both father and mother to his children. He called Thérèse his "little queen" and often took her walking or fishing in the surrounding countryside. Her character had changed: the shock of her mother's death had turned her into an introverted, shy and self-effacing child. Her entry into the Benedictine Abbey school of Notre-Dame du Pré was a trial for her: "The five years (1881-1886) I spent there were the saddest of my life". She worked hard, and loved catechism, history and science, but had trouble with spelling and mathematics.

At the age of ten, she was deeply distressed when Pauline, her favourite sister whom she had chosen as a substitute mother, left to become a Carmelite (2 October 1882). This new emotional shock went so deep that she fell seriously ill. For a whole month, her family were at their wits' end: even doctors could find no explanation for the hallucinations, tossings, turnings and anorexia which afflicted her. Family and Carmelites alike prayed to Our Lady of Victories. And, on 13 May 1883, when it seemed that she would either die or lose her sanity, the family's statue of the Virgin smiled at her, and she was cured. But "spiritual torment" was to be her lot for years to come, slackening only when she started preparing for her long-awaited First Communion. At the age of eleven, on 8 May 1884, she received her first "kiss of love", a sense of being "united" with Jesus, of His giving Himself to her, as she gave herself to Him. Her eucharistic hunger made her long for daily communion. Confirmation, "the sacrament of Love", which she received on 14 June 1884 filled her with ecstasy. Holidays in Trouville and Saint-Ouen-le-Pin were followed, however, by a retreat which triggered a crisis of scru-

ples, lasting seventeen months. Her sister, Marie, helped her to overcome it. But Marie in her turn entered the Lisieux Carmel on 15 October 1886. This was too much for the adolescent Thérèse, who had now lost a third mother. She was nearly fourteen and already strikingly good-looking, 1.62 metres tall with magnificent eyes and long hair. She attracted notice on the beach in Trouville, where people nicknamed her "the tall English girl". But she was tormented by an inner anguish which found relief only when, in November 1886, she appealed to her four brothers and sisters in heaven to intercede for her. Even then, she remained hypersensitive, weak-willed, "crying at having cried". How could she possibly enter the Carmel - something she had dreamed of since the age of nine as a way of living with Jesus - in this pitiful state?

The Garden in the Carmel

The Christmas conversion

Grace intervened to change her life as she was going up the stairs at Les Buissonnets on her return from Midnight Mass at Saint Peter's Cathedral on 25 December 1886. Something her father said provoked a sudden inner change. The Holy Child's strength supplanted her weakness. The strong character she had had at the age of four and a half was suddenly restored to her. A ten-year struggle had ended. Her tears had dried up. Freed at last from herself, she embarked on her "Giant's Race". "My heart was filled with charity. I forgot myself to please others and, in doing so, became happy myself". Now, she could fulfil her dream of entering the Carmel as soon as possible to love Jesus and pray for sinners. Grace received at Mass in Summer 1887 left her with a vision of standing at the foot of the Cross, collecting the blood of Jesus and giving it to souls. Having heard people speak of the three murders committed by a certain Pranzini, she decided to save him from hell through prayer and sacrifice. On 1 September 1887, she wept for joy : just before being guillotined, the prisoner kissed the crucifix. For Thérèse, her "first child" had obtained God's mercy. She hoped that many others would follow once she was in the Carmel.

For Thérèse, 1887 was a year of global development - physical, intellectual, artistic and especially spiritual. With the stubbornness of a woman in love, she fought to enter the Carmel at the age of fifteen. She had to overcome the opposition of her father (easily persuaded), her uncle Guérin, the bursar of the Carmel and Monseigneur Hugonin, the Bishop of Bayeux... So, during the pilgrimage to Italy with her father and sister Céline, she decided to approach Leo XIII himself.

This month of November 1887, when she discovered Switzerland, Florence, Venice, Assisi and above all Rome, marked a turning point in her life. She looked and listened eagerly, now realising that priests were not angels, but "weak and fragile human beings", greatly in need of prayer. She understood better just what it meant to be a Carmelite. But the aim of her pilgrimage never wavered : to ask the Pope's permission to enter the Carmel at fifteen. According to Céline, the audience, which took place on Sunday 20 November 1887, was a disaster. Leo XIII answered Thérèse's entreaties evasively. The young girl was carried out in tears by the papal guards. Now she only had Jesus to turn to.

Back in Lisieux and after a difficult wait, she finally received Bishop Hugonin's permission. But she still had to be patient a while longer. On Monday 9 April 1888, an emotional and tearful but determined Thérèse Martin said goodbye to Les Buissonnets and her family. She was going to live "for ever and ever" in the desert with Jesus and twenty-four enclosed companions : she was fifteen years and three months old.

In the Carmel (1888-1897)

Sister Thérèse of the Child Jesus was happy with her lot, but everyday life in the Carmel had its problems too : the clashes of communal life, the cold, the new diet and the difficulties of prayer (two hours' prayer and four and a half of liturgy). First a postulant and then a novice, she took the Carmelite habit on 10 January 1889, after a retreat marked by a deep sense of inner barrenness. She had her own good reasons for adding "of the Holy Face" to her name in religion.

WHAT IS CARMEL?

On Mount Carmel in the Holy Land, near the present-day Haifa, one can still see caves where hermits once lived in accordance with the spiritual tradition founded by the Prophet Elijah.

In the 13th century, the hermit brethren came together under a common rule as the "Brothers of the Virgin Mary". The Carmel was born.

*In sixteenth century Spain, **Teresa of Avila** and **John of the Cross** reformed the Carmel radically, simplifying its way of life, emphasising contemplative prayer, solitary work in a strictly enclosed setting and a life of brotherhood, to create small "islands" to pray for the world's salvation. The **Lisieux Carmel** was founded in 1838. When Thérèse Martin entered in 1888, it had 26 sisters (average age 47). They spent six and a half hours praying in the nuns' choir every day (including two hours of communal prayer), worked to earn a meager living and had 2 hours' daily recreation.*

There was severe fasting. All the sisters rose at 5.45 am, even in winter, and went to bed around 11pm.

There are more than 800 Carmelite convents in the world, including 110 in France.

In the meantime, a further shock came on the family front when her beloved father developed cerebral arteriosclerosis and suddenly disappeared from Les Buissonnets in June 1888.

12 February 1889 was a black day for the Martin family: after an attack of dementia, the "Patriarch" was taken to the Bon-Sauveur hospital in Caen. "Oh, I do not think I could have suffered more than I did on that day!!!" Seeing her father's humiliation hurt Thérèse deeply. She began to understand the sufferings of the mocked Christ, the Suffering Servant foretold by Isaiah.

She was also affected by the spiritual atmosphere in the community, which was still tainted by Jansenism and the vision of an avenging God. Some of the sisters feared divine justice and suffered badly from scruples. Even after her general confession in May 1888 to Father Pichon, her Jesuit spiritual director, Thérèse was still uneasy. But a great peace came over her when she at last made her profession on 8 September 1890 - although taking the black veil (a public ceremony) on 24 September was a day "veiled in tears".

It was the reading of St John of the Cross, an unusual choice at the time, which brought her relief. In the *"Spiritual Canticle"* and the *"Living Flame of Love"*, she discovered "the true Saint of Love". This, she felt, was the path she was meant to follow. During a community retreat (October 1891), a Franciscan, Father Alexis Prou, launched her on those "waves of confidence and love", on which she had previously been afraid to venture.

The harsh winter of 1890-1891 and a severe influenza epidemic killed three of the sisters, as well as Mother Geneviève, the Lisieux Carmel's founder and "Saint". Thérèse was spared, and her true energy and strength began to show themselves. She felt immense relief when her father, his mind now that of a child, returned to the Guérin household in May 1892 (the lease on Les Buissonnets had expired at Christmas 1889). Céline stayed at home to look after him, although she, too, was thinking of becoming a Carmelite.

Thérèse was delighted when her sister, Agnès of Jesus (Pauline), was elected prioress in succession to Mother Marie de Gonzague (20/2/1893). Asked by Pauline to write verses and theatrical entertainments for liturgical and community festivals, Thérèse wrote two plays about Saint Joan of Arc, "her beloved sister", performing them herself with great feeling and conviction (1894-95).

Her father's death at the Château de la Musse, the Guérins' home, freed Céline to enter the Lisieux Carmel in September 1894, something she and Thérèse both wanted. She brought her camera with her, using it to enliven recreation periods and incidentally leaving her sister's picture to posterity.

A turning point in Thérèse's spiritual development came in late 1894/early 1895, when two Old Testament texts, found in one of Céline's notebooks, brought years of searching to an end. Aspiring to sanctity but aware of her weakness, she felt unworthy to "climb the steep ladder of holiness". But the arms of Jesus were to lift her instead. While she remained small and "became even smaller", God would take her and turn

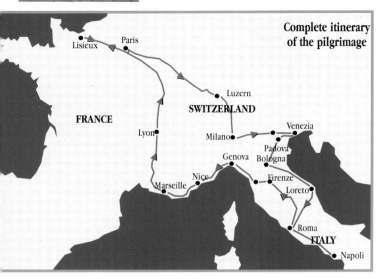

Complete itinerary of the pilgrimage

people the secrets of the "Little Way of Spiritual Childhood", which had already done so much for her (see p. 14-15).

Afflicted for months by a sore throat which stubbornly resisted treatment, Thérèse suffered two haemorrhages during Holy Week of 1896. Far from panicking, she saw this as a summons from her Spouse and looked forward to joining Him soon. But sudden anguish overwhelmed her at Easter and she fell into a dark night of the soul, an "underground labyrinth", a "fog". Heaven seemed to have shut its gates against her. This trial of faith and hope, which made her participate in Christ's Passion, was to last, with a few brief periods of respite, to the end of her life. But she turned the test into a redemptive one, agreeing to remain alone in the darkness so that atheists might receive the Light.

While she was praying in the church that summer, strange and powerful desires started to torment her : she wanted to become a priest, a prophet, a Doctor of the Church, a missionary, a martyr... Chancing on a passage in Saint Paul, she discovered her true vocation at the age of twenty-two : "In the heart of the Church, my Mother, I shall be Love. This way, I shall be everything". Writing down these confidences for her sister and godmother, Marie of the Sacred Heart, in September 1896, she gave the world a spiritual masterpiece (Manuscript B). The wish to "save souls" never left her, and she was seriously thinking of leaving for the Carmel founded in Saigon by the Lisieux sisters.

But tuberculosis was gaining ground undetected. Early in 1897, Thérèse began to feel that "her course would not be a long one". In April, worn out, she was forced to abandon community life, remaining either in her cell or in the garden. In June, Pauline realised that her death was imminent. In a panic, she implored Mother Marie de Gonzague to let Thérèse finish putting down her recollections. Burning with fever, Thérèse wrote a further 36 pages in a little black notebook. Exhausted, she went to the infirmary on 8 July. For a month, she coughed blood, slept little and was unable to eat, while the tuberculosis began to affect her intestines. Doctor de Cornières treated her with the methods of the time, but they could do nothing to help her.

Her sisters took turns keeping vigil at her bedside. Since April, Pauline had been writing down everything she said. More than 850 recorded utterances were later to be published as the *Last Conversations*. In this short work, Thérèse suffers, prays, weeps, makes jokes to distract her sisters and speaks of her own short life.

A prey to constant darkness, she came to understand the temptations of suicide, but lived in trust and love until the very end. She identified herself with the suffering Jesus and offered everything "for sinners". She felt an overwhelming desire "to do good after her death". With great difficulty, she wrote last letters to her spiritual brothers, Fathers Bellière and Roulland.

The appalling pain she suffered wore her out, but she never lost her smile or her deep-seated serenity. A brief remission was followed by a 48-hour agony. She died on Thursday 30 September 1897 whispering : "My God, I love You!" Her face was radiant.

She died unknown, just as she had lived unknown in a provincial Carmel - of tuberculosis, but also of "Love", as she herself had wanted. She wrote to Father Bellière : "I am not dying, I am entering into Life". This was just the beginning...

her into a saint. Inspired by this revelation, her spirit unfolded and soared throughout the year 1895. Having discovered the treasures of God's "Merciful Love", she gave herself to Him at the Mass of the Trinity on 9 June 1895. Without her companions' being aware of it, she reached new mystical heights.

Pauline had recently ordered her to put down her "childhood memories" in writing for her family. Thérèse obeyed and began, in her few spare moments, to "sing God's mercies" to her in her own short life. She saw herself as a "little white flower" which had grown under the rays of the divine sun. In January 1896, she gave her prioress an 86 page notebook (Manuscript A) in which she reinterpreted her life in the light of God's Merciful Love.

The re-election of Mother Marie de Gonzague (21 March 1896), after seven ballots, divided the community. Although Thérèse was herself the youngest novice, the new prioress entrusted the other five novices to her care. In the circumstances, the task was not an easy one, but she performed it with amazing maturity and skill. Two missionary priests, destined for China and Africa, were also entrusted to her. She revealed to these seven young

THÉRÈSE THE WOMAN

"I still cannot understand why women are so easily excommunicated in Italy, for every minute someone was saying: 'Don't enter here... Don't enter there, you will be excommunicated!...'
Ah! Poor women, how they are misunderstood!...

And yet they love God in much larger numbers than men do and, during the Passion of Our Lord, women had more courage than the Apostles since they braved the insults of the soldiers and dared to wipe the adorable face of Jesus... It is undoubtedly because of this that He allows misunderstanding to be their lot on earth, since He chose it for Himself. In heaven, He will show that His thoughts are not men's thoughts, for the last will be the first...

More than once during the trip, I hadn't the patience to wait for heaven to be the first..."

(Ms A, 66ᵛᵒ)

Genealogical Table

Pauline

Léonie

Céline

Marie

THE MARTINS

THE GUÉRINS

Pierre MARTIN
16.4.1777-26.6.1865

Marie-Anne-Fanie BOUREAU
12.1.1800-8.4.1883

Isidore GUÉRIN
6.7.1789-8.9.1868

Louise MACE
11.7.1804-9.9.1859

Married 4 April 1818

Married 5 September 1828

Pierre
Marie-Anne
Anne-Françoise*
Anne-Sophie
(all died in their youth)

Louis
22.8.1823-29.7.1894

Marie-Louise
Sister Marie-Dosithée
Visitandine
(1829-1877)

Zélie
(Marie-Azélie)
23 Dec. 1831-28. Aug. 1877

Isidore
(1841-1909)

Céline
FOURNET
(1847-1900)

Married 13 July 1858

Married
11.9.1866

Marie
Sister Marie
of the Sacred
Heart, Carmelite
in Lisieux
(22 February 1860-
19 January 1940)

Pauline
Sister Agnès
of Jesus,
Carmelite
in Lisieux
(7 September 1861-
28 July 1951)

Léonie
Sister Françoise-
Thérèse,
Visitandine
(3 June 1863-
16 June 1941)

Céline
Sister Geneviève
of the Holy Face,
Carmelite in Lisieux
(28 April 1869-
25 February 1959)

Thérèse
Sister Thérèse
of the Child Jesus
and the Holy Face,
Carmelite in Lisieux
(2 January 1873-
30 September 1897)

Jeanne
(1868-1938)

Marie
Sister Marie
of the
Eucharist,
Carmelite
in Lisieux
(1870-1905)

Paul
died at birth
1871

Three children died
in infancy
Hélène 1864-1870
Joseph-Louis 1866-1867
Joseph Jean-Baptiste 1867-1868

One daughter died
in infancy
Mélanie-Thérèse
16 August-
8. October 1870

* mother of Adolphe Leriche

Servants of God

Louis Martin (1823-94)
and Zélie Guérin (1831-77)
The parents of St Thérèse
of the Child Jesus,
declared "Venerable" by Pope
John Paul II on 26 March 1994

© OCL Lisieux

© OCL Lisieux

"The Good Lord gave me a father and mother more worthy of Heaven than earth"

St Thérèse of the Child Jesus
(Letter 261 dated 26 July 1897)

Proceedings for Canonisation of Thérèse's parents, the "Servants of God" Louis Martin and Zélie Guérin were conducted separately by the dioceses of Bayeux-Lisieux and Sées between 1957 and 1960 and the findings sent to Rome.

Conducted in the traditional manner and referred to Rome in a single study or Positio, the two cases were conducted together. If the Church so decides, Thérèse's father and mother may thus be canonised together.

The faithful are therefore asked to pray jointly to Louis Martin and Zélie Guérin for the granting of favours and miracles through their intercession.

On 26 March 1994, Pope John Paul II declared them "Venerable" and formally recognised their "heroic virtues".

To report favours received, make donations or obtain further information, please write to:
General Postulancy
of the Discalced Carmelites,
Corso d'Italia, 38
00198 Roma (Italy)

Prayer for favours
through the intercession
of the Servants of God
and for their
canonisation:

God our Father,
I thank You for having given us
Louis Martin and Zélie Guérin.
United and faithful
in marriage, they have left us
an example of Christian living
and evangelical virtue.
In raising a large family
through trials, suffering
and bereavement, they put
their trust in You
and always sought to do
Your will.

Deign, Lord,
to make known Your will
in their regard and grant
the favour I ask,
in the hope that the father
and mother of St Thérèse
of the Infant Jesus may one day
be held up by the Church
as a model for the families
of our time.
Amen.

99

CHRONOLOGY

ALENÇON

1873   **2 JANUARY**
Birth of Marie-Françoise
Thérèse Martin
4 JANUARY
Baptism in the Church
of Notre-Dame
MARCH 73 - APRIL 74
Put out to nurse in
Semallé (8 km from
Alençon)

1877   **28 AUGUST**
Death of Zélie Martin

Souvenirs of Thérèse.
Les Buissonnets.

© OCL Lisieux

LISIEUX:
AT THE BUISSONNETS
(1877-1888)

1877   **16 NOVEMBER**
Move to Les Buissonnets

1881   **3 OCTOBER**
Day-boarder at the Bene-
dictine Abbey school of
Notre-Dame du Pré

1882   **2 OCTOBER**
Pauline Martin enters
the Carmel in Lisieux

1883   **25 MARCH**
Thérèse falls gravely ill
13 MAY
She is cured (smile of
the Virgin)

1884   **8 MAY**
First Communion
14 JUNE
Confirmation
administered by
Monseigneur Hugonin

1885   **MAY**
Beginning of crisis
of scruples

1886   **FEBRUARY**
She falls ill and is taken
out of school.
Private tuition.
15 OCTOBER
Marie Martin enters
the Carmel
25 DECEMBER
"Conversion" of Thérèse

1887   **AUGUST**
Prayer for Pranzini
31 OCTOBER
Audience with
Monseigneur Hugonin
in Bayeux
4 NOV.-2 DEC.
Pilgrimage to Italy

1888   **9 APRIL**
She enters the Carmel at
the age of 15 years and
3 months

1888   **23-27 JUNE**
Louis Martin runs away
and is found in Le Havre

AT THE CARMEL
(1888-1897)

1889   **10 JANUARY**
Thérèse takes
the Carmelite habit
12 FEBRUARY
Louis Martin is admitted
to the Bon-Sauveur
hospital in Caen
25 DECEMBER
The lease on Les
Buissonnets is given up

1890   **8 SEPTEMBER**
Thérèse takes her vows
24 SEPTEMBER
Public ceremony
for taking the veil

1891   **OCTOBER**
Retreat conducted
by Father Prou. Thérèse
reads Saint John of
the Cross
WINTER
Severe influenza
epidemic

1892   **10 MAY**
Louis Martin returns
home

1893   **20 FEBRUARY**
Sister Agnès of Jesus
(Pauline Martin) is
elected prioress

1894   **2 JANUARY**
Thérèse turns 21
29 JULY
Louis Martin dies
14 SEPTEMBER
Céline Martin enters
the Carmel
WINTER
On the instructions of
her prioress, Thérèse
starts setting down
her childhood memories.
She discovers the "Little
Way".

1895   Manuscript A is
completed this year

1892. Marie Guérin, Léonie, a servant, Céline, Mr Martin, a servant, Mr and Mrs Guérin, a friend and Thérèse's pet dog: Tom.

AFTER HER DEATH

1895

21 JANUARY
Thérèse performs her second play on Joan of Arc

9 JUNE
Act of Offering to God's Merciful Love

17 OCTOBER
The seminarist Maurice Bellière is entrusted to Thérèse's care

1896

21 MARCH
Mother Marie de Gonzague is elected prioress, she entrusts her five novices to Thérèse

HOLY THURSDAY
First haemorrhage

EASTER TIME
She enters the "dark night of faith and hope"

30 MAY
Father Roulland is entrusted to her as her second spiritual brother

SEPTEMBER
Thérèse writes letters (Ms B) for Sister Marie of the Sacred Heart: "My vocation is Love!"

1897

APRIL
Thérèse falls seriously ill. (Last Conversations)

JUNE
On her prioress's instructions, she writes Manuscript C

8 JULY
She enters the infirmary

30 JULY
She receives the Last Rites

30 SEPTEMBER
She dies around 7 pm after a prolonged agony

4 OCTOBER
Thérèse is buried in the Lisieux cemetery

1898

30 SEPTEMBER
Her book **"Story of a Soul"** is published in 2 000 copies

1899-1900 First pilgrims to Thérèse's grave: first miracles

1910 First steps in canonisation

1915 Apostolic proceedings begin in Bayeux

1921 Benedict XV promulgates the decree on the heroic virtues of the Venerable Servant of God

1923 The relics are moved to the Carmel

29 APRIL
She is beatified by Pius XI

1925

17 MAY
She is canonised in Rome by Pius XI (500 000 pilgrims)

1927

14 DECEMBER
Pius XI makes Thérèse Patron Saint of Universal Missions with Saint Francis Xavier

1929

30 SEPTEMBER
The first stone is laid for the basilica in Lisieux

1937

11 JULY
The basilica is inaugurated

1941

24 JULY
Foundation of the Mission to France. Its seminary is in Lisieux

1944

3 MAY
Pius XII proclams Thérèse Second Patron Saint of France

1947 Fiftieth anniversary of Thérèse's death. Her relics are taken to nearly all the dioceses in France

1956 Facsimile edition of the **"Autobiographical Manuscripts"** (originals of **"Story of a Soul"**)

1973 The centenary of her birthday is celebrated

1980

2 JUNE
John Paul II goes on a pilgrimage to Lisieux

1971-1988 The **"Centenary Edition"** (the critical edition of Thérèse's **"Complete Works"** is published

1992 The **New Centenary Edition"** is published and presented to John Paul II on 18/2/1993

...
around 1997 Celebration of Thérèse's "Entry into Life" in Lisieux and worldwide...

Construction of the Basilica.

"How quickly those sunny childhood years slipped away, but what a sweet imprint they left on my soul!"

(Ms A, 11ᵛᵒ)

What she wrote, what she thought...

How did Sister Thérèse of the Child Jesus become known in the world?

© Cerf/Loose

© OCL Lisieux

HER THOUGHTS

This question is often asked, and the answer is: through a book... which she never wanted to write! This sounds like a paradox, but it is the simple truth.

On 30 September 1898, a year to the day after Thérèse's death, Mother Agnès of Jesus and Mother Marie de Gonzague, who was now prioress, published an exceptionally long memorial circular (476 pages!) and sent it to all the Carmels in France. The surplus was sold (2 000 copies at 4 francs each).

Mother Agnès had in fact collected all the manuscripts (later known as A, B and C) which her sister had been ordered to write, corrected the (many) spelling mistakes, tidied up the text, made some deletions and divided the whole text into chapters. Of the three addressees, only one was named - Mother Marie de Gonzague, on her own insistence. Some poems and letters by Thérèse were added. The Carmel expected to lose money on the book, which uncle Guérin had generously but unenthusiastically agreed to finance. To everybody's surprise, a second edition was needed six months later (4 000) and a third one soon after that... It became a runaway success. By

1956, more than 40 editions had been published, excluding translations, of which the first appeared in 1901. Officially, there have been more than 50 of these, but the real figure is certainly much higher, because of pirate editions.

This book rapidly became an instrument of conversion and healing, inspiring fervent pilgrims from all over the world to come and pray at the "little saint's" grave in the cemetery at Lisieux. A guard was soon needed to protect it against unwitting damage by the faithful.

It was only in 1956, after the death of Mother Agnès, who had virtually rewritten her sister's texts, that Pius XII ordered publication of the three original manuscripts.

The critical edition, prepared and published in phototype by Father François of Saint Marie (who died in 1961) and a team of Lisieux Carmelites, was a momentous event. At long last, the real Thérèse was revealed instead of the old sugary version.

A new team took over in 1969 and produced critical editions of the 266 known letters, 54 poems (1979), 8 plays (1985) and the *Last Conversations* (1971).

This work (1969-1988) was awarded the Grand Prix Cardinal Grente by the Académie Française

in 1989 and culminated in the eight-volume *New Centenary Edition* (Cerf-DDB).

The single-edition of the *Complete Works* (Cerf-DDB) runs to 1600 pages, printed on thin paper. It was presented to John Paul II on 18 February 1993.

(See bibliography on last page).

The two-volume record of the *Beatification and Canonisation Proceedings* is available from the O.C.L. It was published in Rome, in French, in 1973 and 1976.

"Story of a Soul" made Thérèse known throughout the world.

"My 'little way' as you call it..."

A Solitary Journey

Thérèse Martin's spiritual journey was a solitary one. It is true that her family, her teachers and her directors in the Carmel gave her a great deal - but no priest marked her deeply. Her own spiritual director, Father Pichon, was far away in Canada. In her, the Holy Spirit mapped out a way of truth - "I have never looked for anything but the truth" - showing her the depths of the Trinity's Love and a "way" of uniting herself with it which had nothing to do with classroom learning: all of it was rooted in everyday life. It was, of course, providential that her prioress asked her to record her life in writing and entrusted novices to her care, thus revealing a spirituality unparalleled in one so young.

Her incomparable contribution to twentieth-century spirituality was a return to the Gospel in its purest form. "If ye do not become like little children, ye shall not enter the Kingdom of Heaven" (Matthew 18,3). Although she did not know the whole Old Testament, she encouraged people to go back to the Word of God. Without being in any sense a biblical scholar, she quotes the Bible more than 1000 times in her writings.

It was only at the age of 22, that two Old Testament texts brought a long period of searching to an end: showing her the "Way of Spiritual Infancy", which was to symbolise her own contribution. As a young girl, she eagerly sought holiness ("I **must** become a saint" she wrote in 1888), but was repeatedly frustrated by her own helplessness and weakness. After reading in St John of the Cross that God never inspires a wish that cannot be fulfilled, she found fresh courage after seven years of religious life. Unable to "climb the steep ladder of perfection" on her own, she received an unexpected "lift" to her Father: through Jesus' arms (1895).

Conscious of her own weakness, but boldly trusting in God's Merciful Love, which finds its way even to the humble, she came to love her poverty.

Her desire was "to be small and become even smaller". She never reduced her aspirations - they were boundless - but relied on God alone to make them come true. And indeed, she found that He was granting her wishes, small and great.

She had her own incontrovertible logic: God is asking me to do something, I cannot do it on my

afin de vivre dans un acte de parfait Amour, Je m'offre comme Victime d'Holocauste à votre Amour miséricordieux, vous priant de me consumer sans cesse, laissant déborder en mon âme les flots de tendresse infinie qui sont renfermés en vous et que je devienne Martyre de votre Amour, ô mon Dieu!... Que ce martyre après m'avoir préparée à paraître devant vous me fasse enfin mourir et que mon âme s'élance sans retard dans l'Éternel embrassement de Votre Miséricordieux Amour. Je veux, ô mon Bien-Aimé, à chaque battement de mon cœur vous renouveler cette offrande un nombre infini de fois, jusqu'à ce que les ombres s'évanouissant et qu'alors je puisse vous redire mon Amour dans un Face à Face éternel!...

own, so He will do it for me. Her Offering of herself to Merciful Love begins with these words (9 June 1895):

"I desire to be a saint, but I feel my helplessness and I beg you, O my God! to be Yourself my Sanctity!".

From then on and in all circumstances, she lived the daring surrender of herself. For a wholly dependent child has no choice but to abandon itself completely to its father's merciful love. There was no risk of regressing into childishness, for Christmas Eve 1886 had taught Thérèse what it meant to "emerge from the swaddling-clothes of infancy". But she rediscovered the truth of Jesus' stern words: "If ye do not become as little children, ye shall not enter the Kingdom of Heaven" (Mt 18,3), for the way of spiritual infancy is Jesus' own way as a son - the supreme son, living only for his Father. Who is more fully an adult than Jesus? Who is more fully a child?

From that moment on, Thérèse lost her fear of sin, of falling asleep during prayer or any other imperfection - Love had burned everything away. She placed no reliance on her own good works - many as they were - but only on God's freely given Love. "I shall appear before You with empty hands, for I do not ask you, Lord, to count my works."

Her intuitions anticipate the great truths brought to light again by the Second Vatican Council: the primacy of **Jesus'** pascal mystery over all individual devotions, the sense of holiness as something offered to every baptised person, a **devotion to Mary** which sees her, from the depths of a tried and tested faith, more as mother than queen (see the poem *Why I love thee, O Mary,* May 1897), an **ecclesiology** of communion founded on the presence of Love (the Holy Spirit) at the heart of the Church, giving life to all vocations within the Communion of Saints in Heaven and on Earth.

Her vision of her own last end was revolutionary too: not rest but action: "I will spend my heaven doing good on earth".

Without realising it, Thérèse opened ways to ecumenism: her reading of the Epistle to the Romans appeals to Lutherans, while Orthodox Christians put her on a par with Saint Francis of Assisi. The universal symbols used by both saints makes it easy for other civilisations to accept them.

© OCL Lisieux

"Oh, dear Sister, I beg you, understand your little girl, understand that to love Jesus, to be His victim of love, the weaker one is, without desires or virtues, the more suited one is for the workings of this consuming and transforming Love… The desire alone to be a victim suffices, but we must consent to remain always poor and without strength, and this is the difficulty, for: 'The truly poor in spirit, where do we find him? You must look for him from afar,' said the psalmist. … He does not say that you must look for him among great souls, but 'from afar,' that is to say in lowliness, in nothingness. … Ah! let us remain then very far from all that sparkles, let us love our littleness, let us love to feel nothing, then we shall be poor in spirit, and Jesus will come to look for us, and however far we may be, He will transform us into flames of love…

Oh! how I would like to be able to make you understand what I feel!… It is confidence and nothing but confidence that must lead us to Love. … Does not fear lead to Justice?… Since we see the way, let us run together. Yes, I feel it, Jesus wills to give us the same graces, He wills to give us His heaven gratuitously."

- *(Letter 197)* -   *(ICS Publications)*

"Ah! In spite of my littleness, I want to enlighten souls as did the Prophets and Doctors. I have the vocation of an Apostle… I would like to travel over the whole earth to preach Your Name and to plant Your Glorious Cross on foreign soil. But O my Beloved, one mission alone would not be sufficient for me. I want to preach the Gospel on all the five continents simultaneously and even on the most remote isles… I want to be a missionary, not for a few years only, but from the beginning of creation until the consummation of the ages… But above all, O my Beloved Saviour, I want to shed my blood for You even to the very last drop…"

- *(Ms B, 3ro)* -

Thérèse and the priesthood

On the eve of her Profession, Thérèse solemnly declared:
"I came (to the Carmel) to save souls and most of all, to pray for priests"
(Ms A, 69v°).

A few days before she died, she confided:
*"Yes, I wish to spend my heaven doing good on earth (17 July 1897)…
I will help priests, missionaries, the whole Church (13 July 1897) ".*

This is why, in the wake of the two "spiritual brothers" entrusted to her care in 1895 and 1896, many priests have sought her protection and tried to follow in her path.

The first "spiritual brother", Father Maurice Bellière, a 21-year old seminarist, asked her to pray for his vocation. He became a "White Father" and went to Nyasaland (now Malawi), before returning to France, where he died, at the age of 33, in the Bon Sauveur hospital at Caen in 1907. Thérèse's correspondence helped him greatly. She wrote him eleven important letters.

The second, Father Adolphe Roulland, of the Paris Foreign Missions, went to Su-tchuen in China and began corresponding with Thérèse, having celebrated his first Mass in the Lisieux Carmel and talked to her sister. She wrote him six letters. He died in France in 1934.
Her contacts with these two young priests broadened Thérèse's horizons to take in the whole world. Even when she was seriously ill, she remained deeply conscious of her own missionary role.

After her death, many priests and nuns found their vocations when they encountered Thérèse. She kept her promise. A host of priests and missionaries placed their ministry under her protection.

Founded in 1929, the Sacerdotal Union of Saint Thérèse of Lisieux brings together priests from all over the world, who follow her path, entrusting themselves and their ministry to her.

The statutes of the Sacerdotal Union can be obtained from:
PELERINAGE
33, RUE DU CARMEL
14102 – LISIEUX CEDEX

Adolphe Roulland

Maurice Bellière

PRAYER FOR FATHER BELLIÈRE

O my Jesus! I thank You for fulfilling one of my dearest wishes, that of having a brother priest and apostle… I feel very unworthy of this favour but, as You deign to give Your poor little spouse the grace to work specially for the sanctification of a soul destined for the priesthood, I gladly offer You, for that soul, all the prayers and sacrifices of which I am capable; I ask You, O my God, to not look at what I am, but what I should and want to be, a nun wholly consumed by the fire of Your love.

You know, Lord, that my sole ambition is to make You known and loved; and now my wish will be fulfilled. I can only pray and suffer, but the soul with which You deign to unite me through the sweet bonds of charity will go down onto the plain as a warrior to win hearts for You, and I, on the Mount of Carmel, will implore You to give him victory.

Divine Jesus, hear my prayer for the one who wishes to become Your missionary, keep him safe amidst the dangers of the world, make him feel increasingly the emptiness and vanity of passing things and the happiness of disdaining them for love of You. Let his sublime apostolate already work on those around him, let him be an apostle worthy of Your Sacred Heart… O Mary! Sweet Queen of Carmel, to Your care I entrust the soul of this future priest, whose unworthy little sister I am. Deign to show him the love with which You touched the Holy Infant Jesus and dressed Him in swaddling clothes, so that He may one day ascend to the Sacred Altar and bear the King of Heaven in his hands.

I also beseech You to keep him always within the shadow of Your Virgin's cloak, until the happy day when, leaving this vale of tears behind, he beholds Your splendour and enjoys, for all eternity, the fruits of his glorious apostolate…

Thérèse of the Child Jesus (between 17 and 21 October 1895); Prayer nr. 8

Discovering her vocation

"Then, in the excess of my delirious joy, I cried out: O Jesus my Love... my vocation, at last I have found it, my vocation is Love!... Yes, I have found my place in the Church and it is You, O my God, who have given me this place... In the heart of the Church, my Mother, I shall be Love... thus I shall be everything... and thus my dream will be realised!!!...« (Ms B, 3ᵛᵒ)

"Considering the mystical body of the Church, I did not recognise myself in any of the members described by St Paul, or rather I desired to see myself in them *all*... Charity gave me the key to my *vocation*. I understood that if the Church had a body composed of different members, the most necessary and most noble of all could not be lacking to it, and so I understood that the Church had a heart and that this Heart was burning with Love. I understood it was Love alone that made the Church's members act, that if Love ever became extinct, apostles would not preach the Gospel and martyrs would not shed their blood... I understood that *Love* comprised all times and places... in a word, that it was eternal!...

Then, in the excess of my delirious joy, I cried out: O Jesus my Love... my vocation, at last I have found it, my vocation is Love!... Yes, I have found my place in the Church and it is You, O my God, who have given me this place... In the heart of the Church, my Mother, I shall be Love... thus I shall be everything... and thus my dream will be realised!!!..." (Ms B, 3ᵛᵒ)

"I don't hasten to the first place but to the last; rather than advance myself like the Pharisee, I repeat, filled with confidence, the publican's humble prayer. Most of all, I imitate the conduct of Magdalene; her astonishing or rather her loving audacity, which charms the heart of Jesus, also attracts my own. Yes, I feel it; even though I had on my conscience all the sins that can be committed, I would go, my heart broken with sorrow, and throw myself into Jesus' arms, for I know how much He loves the prodigal child who returns to Him. It is not because God, in His *anticipating* Mercy, has preserved my soul from mortal sin that I go to Him with confidence and love".

(End of Ms C)

Marie-Madeleine. Solesmes Abbey.

The trial of faith

Icon

*At Easter time 1896,
Thérèse sank into a darkness
which lasted the eighteen months
leading up to her death.
She accepted this darkness
so that unbelievers might see the light.*

".... then suddenly the fog which surrounds me becomes more dense;
it penetrates my soul and envelops it in such a way that it is impossible
to discover within it the sweet image of my Fatherland, everything has disappeared!
When I want to rest my heart, fatigued by the darkness which surrounds it,
by remembering the luminous country to which I aspire, my torment redoubles;
it seems that the darkness, borrowing the voice of sinners, says mockingly to me:
- You are dreaming about the light, about a fatherland embalmed
in the sweetest perfumes; you are dreaming about the eternal possession
of the Creator of all these marvels; you believe that one day you will walk out
of this fog which surrounds you! Advance, advance; rejoice in death
which will give you not what you hope for but a night still more profound,
the night of nothingness".

"Dear Mother, the image I tried to give you of the darkness
that obscures my soul is as imperfect as a sketch is to the model;
however, I don't want to write any longer about it; I fear I might blaspheme…
I fear that I have already said too much…

Ah! May Jesus pardon me if I have caused Him any pain,
but He knows very well that while I do not have the joy of faith,
I am trying to carry out its work at least. I believe I have made more acts of faith
in this past year than throughout my whole life".
(Ms C, 6vo-7ro)

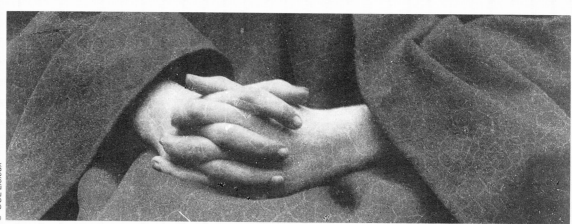

My Joy!

Happiness - people search for it
In vain; it's not on earthly ground:
With me, it's quite the opposite -
It's in my heart that joy is found.
This joy - don't think it comes and goes:
Coming to me, it came to stay.
Delighting, like a fresh spring rose
It smiles upon me every day.

Truly! I'm far too happy, for
It's my own will I always do…
How could I not be joyous, or
Not let my gaiety shine through?…
My joy's from love of suffering,
And, though with tears these eyes are blind,
I smile. I'm truly welcoming
Thorns with the flowers intertwined.

When Heaven's blue grows dark, and so
Seems to have left me cast aside,
My joy's to see myself brought low -
To stay within the shade, to hide.
My joy's His Holy Will (so dear
Is Jesus!) - that I shall obey:
And so I live devoid of fear:
I love the night as much as day.

My joy comes, too, from staying small;
And when I trip upon a stone,
I get up quick. For when I fall
He takes my hand into His own!
Then, cov'ring Him with my caress,
To Jesus: 'You're my All' I say.
I give Him twice the tenderness
As, from my Faith, He slips away.

If, sometimes, tears pour out, it's been
My joy that I've been hiding those:
Oh, suffering has charms: between,
A veil of flowers I interpose!
To suffer silently, so I'll
Give Jesus comfort - that's my will.
My joy comes when I see Him smile,
When I am here in exile still.

My joy is striving that I'll bring
Children of Heav'n to birth (it is
Heart-tender flame!) - through whispering
Over to Jesus, often, this:
"For You (small Brother and Divine!)
I'll suffer; I am happy to.
The only earthly joy of mine -
That I can give delight to You.

"Long as I want my life to be
If that's what You desire, yet, too -
If it would please You, this from me,
To Heav'n I'd like to follow You.
Love's ceaseless fire consumes, from where
My soul has Home - in Heav'n above
It's death? it's life? - I do not care!
Jesus, my joy's to give You love."

21 January 1897 (PN 45)

Courtesy of Alan Bancroft
from a book to be published soon:
Poems of St Thérèse of Lisieux

111

Cures

The Lisieux Carmel has received
— and still receives - thousands of reports
of cures like the ones described below.
And not everybody who is cured
thinks of writing.

PIERRE QUENNEVILLE (1982, Montréal, Canada)

"I am married and have a young child. I had to go into hospital on 22 June last for an operation on a cyst complicated by an infected abcess, which was causing me atrocious pain. I also had bad diabetes and chronic polyneuritis. I could not remain standing for more than half-a-minute. On 15 July, I called Brother Dominic of Jesus. He asked me if I believed in the 'little Thérèse'. I said that I did, and added that I had always tried to follow her spiritual way. He advised me to put a medal of her on each of my legs and to pray for a cure. It was 9.30 in the evening when my wife put the medals on my legs, and I went to Thérèse's shrine in my wheelchair and began praying. I turned to my wife, who asked me : 'Do you have faith?' I answered that I had. 'Then walk.' I got out of the wheelchair immediately and started to walk calmly, although I was afraid that the intense pain would come back. After a few minutes, a sudden warmth came over me, and a wave of emotion. I no longer understood what was happening, I was happy, but still afraid of spoiling everything by letting my emotions take over. I went to thank God on my knees at the shrine, and could not get over my amazement. It all happened at 9.40 in the evening. Since then, I have been walking, and I am getting better. I accept the diabetes as my personal cross, made to measure by God especially for me."

P.B. (Toulon)

"I am writing to you because I vowed to tell people about the two miracles which happened in my family. I am the mother of two sons, and their health has been a torment to me. My elder son was in a coma for three months after a car crash, and all the doctors in the intensive care unit had given him up. We prayed to Saint Thérèse to keep him with us, and she heard our prayers. In September, my youngest was left completely paralysed within twenty minutes by a terrible virus. The doctors gave him no chance of surviving. He spent five and a half months in intensive care, on an artificial lung... Again our prayers were answered and, at the end of six months, a miracle happened and he began talking and walking again. The doctors themselves were amazed."

A. FAUQUET (Lisieux, 12 December 1908)

"I testify that, since 1 January 1906, my 4 1/2 year-old daughter Reine had been suffering from an eye disease, which the doctors told us was incurable. After sixteen months of useless treatment, my wife took our blind child to Saint Thérèse's grave and we began making a novena to the little saint. After only two days, while my wife was at six o'clock Mass, my little Reine suddenly regained her sight after a violent crisis. My wife noticed it first, and I did later. In testimony of which, and with deep gratitude for the miracle worked in our favour, we are signing this certificate in the presence of witnesses." (There follow 11 signatures, and notes added by the doctor who had diagnosed phlyctenular keratitis).

F.X.G. (1980)

"I first heard about Saint Thérèse in 1966, at a time when I was having political problems with the authorities in my country. But the memory soon faded, because I only knew her by name. In 1973, however, the centenary of her birth, I was suffering from a terrible disease called sarcoidosis, and hit on the idea of making a pilgrimage to Lisieux. That was in August. I prayed with all my heart to Saint Thérèse to cure me and I think she heard me, because, nine months later, my doctor told me that I was cured for good."

M.M. (1993)

"I was taking various tranquillisers as a safety measure, having tried repeatedly - and unsuccessfully - to give them up. But I was hopeful, as I had already managed to cut down the dose.
In July 1992, I prayed to Thérèse in the basilica at Lisieux. Since last October, I have gradually stopped taking the Atarax 25 and some of the Urbanyl 10 which I had been using since my depressions started in April 1978, 14½ years ago. Saint Thérèse granted my wish to stop being dependent on these tranquillisers. The depression has gone, even if my memory is not as good as it used to be and I still sleep badly." (A prescription from November 1991 is enclosed, listing eight different medicines).

© OCL Lisieux

The last conversations

*During the last six months of Thérèse's life,
Mother Agnès of Jesus (Pauline) wrote down the last things
her sick and then dying sister said. These 850 utterances
("The last Conversations", published by ICS)
show us a woman who is ill, simple, human, courageous,
gay, concerned about others, sometimes downhearted,
and very close to all victims of serious illness.*

■ 15 MAY 1897

I no longer find anything in books, apart from the Gospel. That book is enough for me... After all, I do not mind if I live or die. I do not really see what more I shall have after death than I already have in this life. It is true that I will see the Good Lord! But I am already completely with him here on earth.

■ 20 MAY

They tell me death will frighten me. It is quite possible that it will. No one distrusts their emotions more than I do. I never rely on my own thoughts; I know how weak I am. But I want to enjoy the feeling God is giving me now. There will be plenty of time to suffer its opposite later.

■ ... JUNE

It is certainly a great grace to receive the sacraments; but it is alright, too, when the Good Lord does not allow it - everything is grace.
- *Life is sad!*
- Exile is sad, not life, said she. "Life" is a beautiful word, and we ought to keep it to what must never die; and, as we already enjoy it since this world, life is not sad, but full of joy!

■ 23 JUNE

Even if I had done everything Saint Paul did, I would still think myself a "useless servant", but it is precisely this that makes me happy for, since I have nothing, God will give me everything.

■ 21 JULY

What does it matter to me whether it is I or somebody else who shows this Way to others; provided it is shown, what does it matter who shows it!

■ 21 JULY

... I ask you humbly: what is truth? Let me see things as they are, let nothing throw dust in my eyes.

■ 30 JULY

(Continuous hemorrhaging, choking for breath. She is not expected to survive the night.)
- *It is dreadful to suffer so much, it must stop you even from thinking!*
- No, it still lets me tell God that I love him, I think that is enough.

■ 3 AUGUST

(Severe pain, particularly in her shoulder)
My little sisters, pray for the poor sick who are dying. If only you knew what it is like! How little it takes to lose one's patience! One has to be charitable to everyone... I would never have thought that before.

■ 8 AUGUST

(I told her I would tell people about her virtues later on.)
It is God only you must praise, for there is nothing to praise in my little nothingness.

■ 9 AUGUST

(We told her she was a saint.)
No, I am not a saint; I have never done the actions of a saint. I am a very little soul that God filled with His graces, this is what I am. What I tell you is the truth, you will see it in heaven.

■ ... AUGUST

If only you knew what terrible thoughts obsess me! Pray for me so that I may not hear the demon who wants to convince me of so many lies. The arguments of the worst materialists are forcing themselves on my mind: science is progressing all the time and will end by giving us natural explanations for everything; we shall have mastered everything and solved all the problems we have today, for many discoveries still lie ahead, and so on...

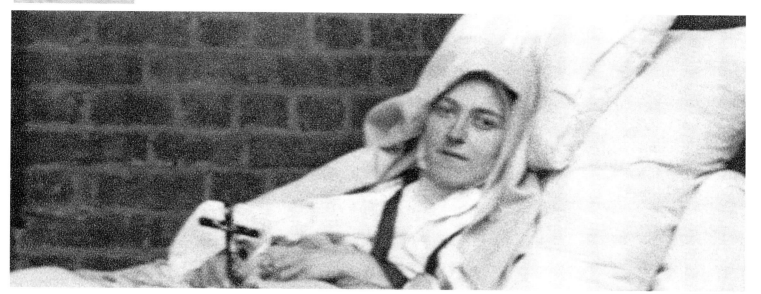

■ 11 AUGUST

(She is getting weaker and thinner all the time.)

I did not expect to suffer so much; I am suffering like a little child... I am too small to have strength from myself.

■ 18 AUGUST

In the weak state in which I am, I wonder how I would react if I suddenly saw a huge spider on the bed. Well, I am sure I could put up with the fright for the Good Lord's sake.

... But what about asking the Virgin not to let it happen?

■ 20 AUGUST

... To think that I always had so much trouble saying the rosary!

■ 28 August

Look at that black hole down there *(under the chestnut trees near the graveyard)*, where you cannot make anything out any more: I am in a hole like that, body and soul. Ah yes, what darkness! But I am at peace in it.

■ 11 SEPTEMBER

I love you so very, very much! When I hear the door opening, I always think it is you; and, when you do not come, I am sad.

Give me a kiss, a kiss that makes a noise, the kind of kiss you can hear!

■ 17 SEPTEMBER

(She spends a sleepless night, racked with coughing)

You have to be cheerful with the sick. Come on, you must not start lamenting, like people who have no hope. *(With a mischievous look on her face)*. You'll finish by making me sorry to go!

■ 22 SEPTEMBER

(She is hardly able to talk any longer).

- What a terrible illness and how you have suffered!
- Yes!!! What a grace it is to believe! If I had not believed in God, I would have killed myself without hesitating.

■ 30 SEPTEMBER

(She was dying. I looked after her during morning Mass. She said nothing to me. She was exhausted, panting for breath: I felt that no words could describe what she was suffering. Joining her hands for a moment, she looked at the statue of the Virgin):

- Oh! I have prayed to her with such fervour! But this is pure agony, with no trace of consolation...

O my dear Blessed Virgin, help me!...

Oh! You know I am suffocating... If only you knew what it is like, not being able to breathe!

... My God, take pity on your poor little girl! Take pity on her! O my mother, I tell you, the chalice is full to the brim!...

... But of course, the Good Lord will not abandon me...

... He has never let me down.

... Yes, my Lord, anything you wish, but have mercy on me!

... My little sisters! My little sisters, pray for me!...

Yes, I think that I have never looked for anything but truth; yes, I have understood the heart's humility... I think that I am humble... Everything I have written about wanting to suffer, oh, it is all true!

... And I do not regret having given myself to Love.

(She died at around 7.20 in the evening).

115

© OCL Lisieux

JE SUIS LE JÉSUS DE THÉRÈSE ...

SI QUELQU'UN EST
TOUT PETIT QU'IL VIENNE À MOI
PROV.

© Cerf/Loose

Pictures held by Thérèse in the photo opposite.

Thérèse on prayer

*"Was it not in prayer that St Paul, St Augustine,
St John of the Cross, St Thomas Aquinas, St Francis,
St Dominic, and so many other famous Friends of God
have drawn on this divine science
which delights the greatest geniuses?
A scholar has said : 'Give me a lever and a fulcrum
and I will lift the world.'
What Archimedes was not able to obtain,
for his request was not directed to God
and was made only from a material viewpoint,
the saints have obtained in all its fullness.
The Almighty has given them as fulcrum : Himself alone;
as lever : prayer which burns with the fire of love.
And it is in this way that they have lifted up the world;
it is in this way that the saints still militant
lift it, and that, until the end of time,
the saints to come will lift it."*
(Ms. C, 36)

*"For me, prayer is an aspiration of the heart,
it is a simple glance directed to heaven,
it is a cry of gratitude and love in the midst of trial
as well as joy. Finally, it is something great and
supernatural, which expands my soul and unites me to Jesus."*
(Ms. C, 25vo)

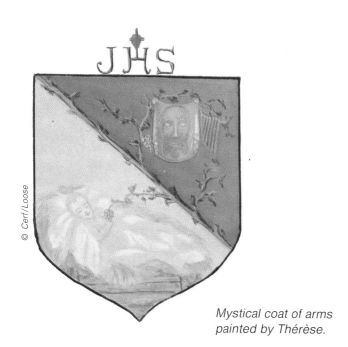

Mystical coat of arms
painted by Thérèse.

"I don't hasten to the first place
but to the last; rather than advance myself
like the Pharisee, I repeat, filled with confidence,
the publican's humble prayer. Most of all, I imitate
the conduct of Magdalene: her astonishing
or rather her loving audacity, which charms
the heart of Jesus, also attracts my own.
Yes, I feel it; even though I had on my conscience
all the sins that can be committed, I would go,
my heart broken with sorrow, and throw myself
into Jesus's arms, for I know how much He loves
the prodigal child who returns to Him.
It is not because God, in His anticipating mercy,
has preserved my soul from mortal sin
that I go to Him with confidence and love."

(End of Ms. C)

Her last cell.

Offering of

At the Mass of the Trinity on 9 June 1895, Thérèse felt inspired to offer herself as a "Holocaust Victim to God's Merciful Love" (and not to God's justice, as was usual at that time), because she had discovered the depths of God's mercy, which reaches down to the humble, poor and wretched. This marks one of the high points of her spiritual life. She was to urge this offering of the self on her sisters and novices. The Church urges it on all the faithful.

Offering of myself as a Holocaust Victim to God's Merciful Love

O my God! Most Blessed Trinity, I desire to love You and make You loved, to work for the glory of the Holy Church by saving souls on earth and liberating those suffering in purgatory. I desire to accomplish Your will perfectly and to reach the degree of glory You have prepared for me in Your Kingdom. I desire, in a word, to be a saint, but I feel my helplessness and I beg You, O my God! to be Yourself my Sanctity!

Since You loved me so much as to give me Your only Son as my Saviour and my Spouse, the infinite treasures of His merits are mine. I offer them to You with gladness, begging You to look upon me only in the Face of Jesus and in His heart burning with Love.

I offer You, too, all the merits of the saints (in heaven and on earth), their acts of Love, and those of the holy angels. Finally, I offer You, O Blessed Trinity! the Love and merits of the Blessed Virgin, my dear Mother. It is to her I abandon my offering, begging her to present it to You. Her Divine Son, my Beloved Spouse, told us in the days of His mortal life, "Whatsoever you ask the Father in my name, he will give it to you!" I am certain, then, that You will grant my desires; I know, O my God! that the more You want to give, the more You make us desire. I feel in my heart immense desires and it is with confidence I ask You to come and take possession of my soul. Ah! I cannot receive Holy Communion as often as I desire, but, Lord, are You not all-powerful? Remain in me as in a tabernacle and never separate Yourself from Your little victim.

I want to console You for the ingratitude of the wicked, and I beg of You to take away my freedom to displease You. If through weakness I sometimes fall, may Your Divine Glance cleanse my soul immediately, consuming all my imperfections like the fire that transforms everything into itself.

118

myself to Love

I thank You, O my God! for all the graces You have granted me, especially the grace of making me pass through the crucible of suffering. It is with joy I shall contemplate You on the Last Day carrying the sceptre of Your Cross. Since You deigned to give me a share in this very precious Cross, I hope in heaven to resemble You and to see shining in my glorified body the sacred stigmata of Your Passion.

After earth's Exile, I hope to go and enjoy You in the Fatherland, but I do not want to lay up merits for heaven. I want to work for Your Love alone, with the one purpose of pleasing You, consoling Your Sacred Heart, and saving souls who will love You eternally.

In the evening of this life, I shall appear before You with empty hands, for I do not ask You, Lord, to count my works. All our justice is stained in Your eyes. I wish, then, to be clothed in Your own Justice and to receive from Your Love the eternal possession of Yourself. I want no other Throne, no other Crown but You, my Beloved!

Time is nothing in Your eyes, and a single day is like a thousand years. You can, then, in one instant prepare me to appear before You.

In order to live in one single act of perfect Love, I offer myself as a victim of Holocaust to Your Merciful Love, asking You to consume me incessantly, allowing the waves of infinite tenderness shut up within You to overflow into my soul, and that thus I may become a martyr of Your Love, O my God!

May this martyrdom, after having prepared me to appear before You, finally cause me to die and may my soul take its flight without any delay into the eternal embrace of Your Merciful Love.

I want, O my Beloved, at each beat of my heart to renew this offering to You an infinite number of times, until the shadows having disappeared, I may be able to tell You of my Love in an Eternal Face to Face!

Marie, Françoise, Thérèse of the Child Jesus and the Holy Face
unworthy Carmelite Religious.
Feast of the Most Holy Trinity
9 June, in the year of grace, 1895.

(ICS Publications)

A universal mission

Even as a child, Thérèse Martin was fascinated by the missions. She lived at a time of epic missionary expansion, which saw hundreds of young priests and nuns leaving for Africa, South America, China and the South Seas...

When, on their journey to Italy, Céline brought her some missionary journals, Thérèse refused to read them : she was too eager to travel to other countries herself to preach the love of Jesus. She felt drawn to the Carmel as a way of doing this, working through prayer and the gift of herself - like her "Spanish Mother", Saint Teresa of Avila - for the conversion of others. Like Teresa, too, "she would have given a thousand lives to save a single soul".

When she entered the Carmel, she said : "I came to save souls and especially to pray for priests". By praying for priests (she had discovered on her Italian pilgrimage that even the holiest priests needed the constant prayers of others), she wanted to become an "apostle of apostles" and so make herself an even more effective missionary.

Increasingly, the whole purpose of her life became "to love Jesus and make Him loved".

She was delighted when she was given two "spiritual brothers" and asked to help them in their ministry : Father Maurice Bellière later became a White Father and missionary in Africa ; Father Adolphe Roulland, of the Paris Foreign Missions, went to China. Thérèse wrote to them until she died and, in so doing, extended her vision of salvation to embrace the whole world (see page 17).

The "immense desires" which tormented her at prayer made her long to "walk the earth" and "proclaim the Gospel on the five continents and the remotest islands..."

"I would be a missionary, not for a few years only, but from the beginning of creation until the consummation of the ages..." (Ms. B, 3ro).

This desire continued growing until she was on her very deathbed, culminating in the hope that she would become an even greater missionary in the life to come. She wrote to Father Roulland : "I will not be inactive in heaven, my desire is to continue working for the Church and souls. I ask this of the Good Lord and I am sure He will grant me this wish." (letter 254).

She repeatedly promised her sisters :
"I will return...", "I will come down..."

The most astonishing thing of all is that, in 1927, the Church actually proclaimed her universal patron saint of the missions.

When her faith was being tried for the last time, she came to realise that her own darkness could bring light to "unbelievers". This was why Cardinal Suhard, Archbishop of Paris - deeply distressed at the general decline of religious faith in France - founded the seminary of the Mission of France in Lisieux in 1941.

Thérèse, the patron saint of missions abroad and at home, never left her cell, but she put so much of the Trinity's Love into her own daily life that she made God's Merciful Love illuminate the world.

The pavillon in Alençon

*More than 50 congregations
in various parts of the world
follow the spiritual path
which she marked out.
Most of them
are apostolic congregations
which have set out
to live in accordance
with her message.
They have about
5000 members.*

The Hermitage in Lisieux

PRAYER TO THÉRÈSE

NOVENA
through the intercession
of Saint Thérèse of the Child Jesus

*God our Father, You welcome to Yourself all those
who serve You faithfully in this world: we call on Saint Thérèse
of the Child Jesus because of the love she bore You.
Her filial trust made her hope that You would do her will
in heaven because she had always done Your will on earth.
Hear, I beseech You, the prayer I address to You
with faith, relying on her intercession.*

Our Father

*Lord Jesus, only Son of God and our Saviour,
remember that Saint Thérèse of the Child Jesus gave her life
here below for the salvation of souls, and wished to spend
her heaven doing good on earth: because she was
Your beloved spouse and ardent in the cause of Your glory,
we pray to her. I entrust myself to You, so that I may obtain
the graces I implore, relying on her intercession.*

Hail Mary

*O Holy Spirit, source of all grace and love, by Your action
Saint Thérèse of the Chid Jesus responded with perfect fidelity
to the divine mercy and blessings which were showered
upon her. Now that she intercedes for us in Heaven,
desiring no respite until the end of time, we implore her aid.*

*I beg You to inspire and hear my prayer, so that I may obtain
the favour I have confided to her intercession.*

Glory be to the Father...

121

Saint Thérèse of Lisieux,
a Doctor of the Universal Church.

This is an official title given to Catholic saints notable for the holiness of their lives, the distinction and orthodoxy of their teaching, and their theological and spiritual learning. This teaching and learning must be of universal relevance. It is the Church, through the Pope, which declares that a saint is a Doctor, following careful examination of a theological and historical file by the Congregations of the Saints and of the Faith.

In response to many requests, and after attentive study, I have the joy to announce that on Mission Sunday, 19 October 1997, in St Peter's Basilica in Rome, I will proclaim St Thérèse of the Child Jesus and the Holy Face a doctor of the Church. In view of this, on 24 August last, during the Angelus prayer in the presence of hundreds of Bishops and before a vast throng of young people from around the world, gathered in Paris for the 12th World Youth Day, I wanted personally to announce my intention to proclaim Thérèse of the Child Jesus and the Holy Face a Doctor of the Universal Church during the celebration of World Mission Sunday in Rome.

Today, 19 October 1997, in St Peter's Square, filled with faithful from every part of the world, and in the presence of a great many Cardinals, Archbishops and Bishops, during the solemn Eucharistic celebration I proclaimed Thérèse of the Child Jesus and the Holy Face a Doctor of the Universal Church.

John Paul II

Until 1970, there were 32 Doctors of the Church, all of them men. That year, Paul VI added two women: Saint Teresa of Avila (1515-1582) and Saint Catherine of Siena (1347-1380).

It is worth noting that Saint Catherine could neither read nor write. She dictated her "Dialogues" and her highly important letters. This shows that a saint does not have to be highly educated or teach in any formal sense to be a Doctor of the Church. Theology (=words about God) is not a matter of speech, but of experience, and this experience is not expressed only in learned treatises. The great women mystics of the Church all have a special place in this heartfelt knowledge of the Divine Mystery, the Mystery of Love.

It is significant that women now figure prominently in the Catechism of the Catholic Church Saint Thérèse of Lisieux is mentioned six times.

She had written in all simplicity and truth: "Ah! If scholars who had spent their lives studying had come to question me, they would certainly have been amazed to see a fourteen year-old child understand the secrets of perfection, secrets which all their learning cannot reveal to them, for only the poor in spirit can possess them!..."(Ms. A, 49r°).

And again, when boundless aspirations were tormenting her, she said: "Ah! In spite of my littleness, I would like to enlighten souls as did the Prophets and the Doctors. I have the vocation of the Apostle..." (Ms B, 3r°).

As nightly, to my joy the votive-flowers are thrown,
Spring roses… as I pull away the petal-leaf,
My only Love! before your Calvary of stone, I'd like to wipe away Your grief..
Throwing of Flowers means "Gather first and bring
All of my lightest sighs and all my deepest woes:
Each little sacrifice-joy, pain as offering -
My flowers are those!"…
Throwing of Flowers - it arms me, Jesus! I'm
certain that when I fight for saving sinners so,
I'll win. By these I will disarm You every time - these flowers, I throw!!

"Throwing of Flowers"
(PN 34).

Courtesy of Alan Bancroft
from a book to be published soon:
Poems of St. Thérèse of Lisieux

The shower of Rose Petals

Thérèse, the "little saint with the roses"… Pilgrims and tourists are sometimes irritated by the often tasteless way in which flowers are heaped round Thérèse in pictures. And yet, if Saint Peter is shown with his keys, Saint Andrew with his cross and Saint Francis of Assisi with the birds of the air, it is only right that Thérèse should be associated with roses. One needs, however, to know why. As a little girl at Les Buissonnets, and later as a Carmelite nun, she had always loved roses, their beauty and their scent. In her earliest childhood, she had joined in strewing rose petals at church festivals: "I loved the feast-days so! (…) I particularly loved the processions of the Blessed Sacrament - what a joy it was to strew flowers before the Lord's feet!… But before letting them fall, I tried to throw them as high as I could, and I was never happier than when my rose petals touched the Holy Monstrance…" (Ms. A, 17r°). When she became mistress of Novices in the Carmel, she taught her charges to do the same. "Every evening in June 1896, after compline, the mistress of novices and her five young charges met before the stone cross in the courtyard at about 8 o'clock. They gathered rose petals from under the twenty or so rosebushes and threw them at Our Lord on the cross: everyone tried to throw higher than the others and to let them touch His Face." (Introduction, PN 34). Thérèse took this all very seriously and sorted through the petals, carefully picking out only the freshest ones. The little girl had become an adult Carmelite, offering her life to God, like the crucified Christ. This is reflected in the canticle she composed for her sister, Mother Agnes of Jesus, on 28 June 1896: Throwing of Flowers.

She put her whole life into these words, as she did into the profound explanation of the rose symbolism which she offered in Manuscript B, written in September 1896. Thérèse explains the meaning of the petals thrown at Jesus, linking this gesture with her recently discovered "Way of Spiritual Infancy".

"Well! I am a child of the Church. This child only knows how to do one thing now, to love You, O Jesus… She is banned from doing great works, from preaching the Gospel, from spilling her blood… But what does it matter, her brothers are working for her, and she, little child, stays close to the throne of the King and Queen, and loves for her brothers who are fighting… But how will she show her love, since love is proven through charitable acts?"

Here is her answer: "I have no other means of proving my love for You than that of strewing flowers, that is, not allowing one little sacrifice to escape, not one look, one word, profiting by all the smallest things and doing them through love; and in this way I shall strew flowers before Your throne. I shall not come upon one without plucking off the petals for You (…) O Jesus, of what use will my flowers be to You? Ah! I know very well that this fragrant shower, these fragile, worthless petals, these songs of love from the littlest of hearts will charm You. Yes, these nothings will please You. They will bring a smile to the Church Triumphant. She will gather up my flowers unpetalled through love and have them pass through Your own divine hands, O Jesus. And this Church in heaven, desirous of playing with her little child, will cast these flowers, which are now infinitely valuable because of Your divine touch, upon the Church Suffering in order to extinguish its flames and upon the Church Militant in order to gain the victory for it!" (Ms. B, 4v°).

Thérèse's roses represent all her acts of love, all her sacrifices, most of them hidden from her sisters. This does not matter, since Jesus sees them. Always clear-headed, Thérèse knows that these little acts are nothing in themselves. But she offers them to the crucified and resurrected Christ. Through this contact with the divine, her worthless acts take on "infinite value". The "shower of roses" (1), which has spread Thérèse's glory across the five continents, can only be understood in this way. Thérèse's roses have power to heal only when they have touched the body of Jesus, the only Saviour. Even when her faith was sorely tried, and she herself was gravely ill, she remained faithful to the gestures of her childhood. The last photograph (August 1897) shows her, painfully thin, strewing rose petals on the crucifix which never left her (VTL 45). A few days before she died, someone brought her a rose; taking each petal separately, she touched Christ's wounds with it, repeating a passage from her canticle, "Strewing Flowers". "As the petals slid from her bed to the infirmary floor, she said very seriously: 'Gather these [rose] petals, little sisters; they will help you to give pleasure later on. Do not lose one of them…'" (CJ 14.9.1). Just one example among many: in 1910, one of these petals healed the gangrenous tongue of Ferdinand Aubry, an inhabitant of Lisieux.

(1) There is a connection here with another theme which becomes steadily more important as Thérèse's death approaches. Sister Mary of the Sacred Heart tells us: "In the refectory, I was reading a life of St Aloysius Gonzaga to the sisters. It said that a sick person, who had prayed to the saint to cure him, saw a shower of roses fall onto his bed, like a symbol of the grace he was about to receive. 'I will do that too', Thérèse said to me during recreation afterwards, after my death, I will send down a shower of roses". (cf. D.E. 9 June).

She identified herself with the rose when she was very ill:
"A rose which has lost its petals",
canticle written on 9 May 1897 (PN 51).

THE SAINTS

*F*rancis
of Assisi

An Unforgettable Man

"Why you? Why you? Why you?" So spluttered good Br. Masseo the question when he wanted his father in religion to explain, once and for all, what people found so special about him. The other remained calm, and only sought the reason for the urgent inquiry. "I mean," said the exasperated Masseo, "why does the whole world run after you? Why does everyone demand to see you, listen to you and obey you? Your face is not beautiful, you are neither full of wisdom nor of noble heritage. Why is it then, that the whole world runs after you?"

That conversation took place almost eight hundred years ago. Even then, Br. Masseo could have spared himself his agitation. Once in a while, persons appear who touch the deeply-seated longings of their contemporaries to such a degree that they can hardly ward off the demands made of them. Of course, when the demands continue for centuries, the usual hubbub around celebrities no longer explains the situation. In such a case, something else enters the picture, something which endures beyond the spirit of an age or the taste of the time. It endures because it constitutes part of being human. It is the dream of a new humanity. In Francis of Assisi (1181-1226), this dream came to fulfillment. In him and in his life, one sees how a completely average person can stand before God and the world and become another expression of what we usually consider human. If it is not extreme to see the Little Poor Man of Assisi as a religious genius, it is crucial to seek this genius not in limited areas of giftedness, but solely in the radical and consistent nature of his devotion to God. "In European intellectual history, Francis of Assisi, because of the purity of his heart and his all encompassing love, is honored by Christians and atheists, skeptics and agnostics, humanists and mystics, poets and artists as the ideal figure of the highest form of humanity." (Xaver Schnieper).

Naturally, there are Christians, atheists, skeptics and agnostics; humanists, mystics, poets and artists who think little or nothing about Francis of Assisi. They may not even know him. That must be said. Otherwise one might imagine this saint of the high middle ages as the irresistible heartbreaker of all time. He is as little that as is his Lord and Master, whose footpints he sought to follow through his life. As the Master, Francis of Assisi cannot be forgotten once one hat truly come to know him. His personality contained something incomparable and unforgettable. Even a brief look at his lige shows how much he followed a new path.

First of all, we see the carefree son of Pietro and Picca Bernadone lacked neither the humor or money to play the King among his peers. In Assisi he set the tone and the group followed. There was little modesty or self-criticism. Later, when he looked back, he described this time as "while I was still in sin." He probably used this expression because everything revolved around his ego.

Then came imprisonment in Perugia between 1202 and 1203. Here began his seven-year-long conversion, the end of wihich saw the birth of a new Francis. This period contains indications of the inner transformation necessary before the little gluttonous caterpillar could become a butterfly. Here he underwent insecurity about and distancing from his past: his flight from the military march to Apulia when he reached Spoleto; his reassessment of all his values after meeting the leper; a new direction after prayer in San Damiano; then burning all bridges by renouncing all claim to his parternal inheritance; and finally, on February 24, 1209; in the Portiuncula, attaining clarity about his further path while hearing the Gospel about the sending out of the disciples.

Then came ten happy years in the life of this "man from another world," as his contemporaries soon experienced him. Irresistible, he went his way, poor as a beggar, but full of joy; touched by Christ, yet open to the world, totally catholic but connected to the whole universe. Soon the first friars joined him. Together, they walked to Rome to attain permission from the "Lord Pope" to live in poverty as wandering preachers. On Palm Sunday of 1212, the daughter of a count, Clare Offreduccio de Favarone, came to the "Penitents of the City of Assisi" and asked for acceptance into their community. Missionary attempts failed in Dalmatia and Spain. Finally, in 1219, Francis wandered farther into the East, where this holy fool of God met the Sultan Melek el Kamil at the Nile Delta, to convert him to Christ. Althoungh, the Sultan remained a Moslem, he nonetheless marveled at this Christian, who was so different from all the rest.

At the beginning of 1220 this traveler to the East returned to Italy and began to notice that many of the friars did not want what he wanted: his complete poverty, his lived humility and penance without thought of achievement. Influential circles in the brotherhood, which already numbered thousands of members, wanted the things of other orders: tight organization, figures of authority, houses of study, etc... Rome also wanted from him and official Rule. For the saint, difficult years had begun, from which only death would free him. In 1223, Pope Honorius III confirmed the definitive Rule, the manger scene at Greccio took place and the saint received the wounds of the Lord on Mount La Verna. The summer of 1225 saw the composition of the famous "Canticle of Brother Sun" and on October 3, 1226, "Sister Death" came to lead him to Christ—the goal of all his longings.

Thus the four phases of the forty-four years allowed the saint give us some small idea of his mystery—the mystery of holy simplicity. We can best understand that mystery if we take a piece of paper and fold it once. The sheet contains one fold, but also has a completely simple, clear meaning. It is obvious what is right and left, above or below. If we were to fold the paper several more times, the edges would begin to fold into rach other, each one losing its strength and clarity. This complicated sheet of paper would become useless because it had lost its one fold—its singleness of meaning. The simplicity of the Gospel that Francis of Assisi lived should not be confused with his lack of needs or a lack of awareness of life's problems. It is much more the concentration of all his strength on what had become his One and all. When this concentration takes place under the influence of a powerful love, we find a breathrough, a decisive step which so readily and easily becomes muddled in all the ifs, ands and buts. Francis of Assisi had none of these hesitations.

Francis Bernadone

Thomas of Celano, his first biographer, testifies:

O how beautiful, how splendid, how glorious did he appear in the innocence of his life, in the simplicity of his words, in the purity of his heart, in his love for God, in his fraternal charity, in his ardent obedience, in his peaceful submission, in his angelic countenance! He was charming in his manners, serene by nature, affable in his conversation, most opportune in his exhortations, most faithful in what was entrusted to him, cautious in counsel, effective in business, gracious in all things. He was serene of mind, sweet of disposition, sober in spirit, raised up in contemplation, zealous in prayer, and in all things fervent. He was constant in purpose, stable in virtue, persevering in grace, and unchanging in all things. He was quick to pardon, slow to become angry, ready of wit, tenacious of memory, subtle in discussion, circumspect in choosing, and in all things simple. He was unbending with himself, understanding toward others, and discreet in all things.

He was a most eloquent man, a man of cheerful countenance, of kindly aspect; he was immune to cowardice, free of insolence. He was of medium height, closer to

shortness; his head was moderate in size and round, his face a bit long and prominent, his forehead smooth and low; his eyes were of moderate size, black and sound; his hair was black, his eyebrows straight, his nose symmetrical, thin and straight; his ears were upright, but small; his temples smooth. His speech was peaceable, fiery and sharp; his voice was strong, sweet, clear, and sonorous. His teeth were set close together, even, and white; his lips were small and thin; his beard black, but not bushy. His neck was slender, his shoulders straight, his arms short, his hands slender, his fingers long, his nails extended; his legs were thin, his feet small. His skin was delicate, his flesh very spare. He wore rough garments, he slept but very briefly, he gave most generously. And because he was very humble, he showed all mildness to all persons, adapting himself usefully to the behavior of all. The more holy amongst the holy, among sinners he was as one of them. Therefore, most holy father, help the sinners, you who loved sinners, and deign, we beg of you, most kindly to raise up by your most glorious intercession those whom you see lying in the mire of their sins (1 Cel 83).

His being is so fashioned; his words, bearing and whole life are so constituted that they form immediate materializations of the Gospel—a literal discipleship, straightforward realization of Jesus's existence without any mitigation or interpretation. Thus Christ's face looks out of his, Christ's bearing becomes clear in his. I know of no one else of whom this can be said.

Here one finds the originality of his mission. No one told him what God wanted of him. No one indicated the content of his life to him. He repeatedly emphasized that God himself, Christ himself had taught him. He knew himself as one taught by God in the truest sense, but without entering into opposition with the authority of the Church as the interpreter of Christ's message.

His life can be understood only as a sacrifice that echoed the deepest loneliness in Christ. His work never became what it could have become. It accepted the limited character all Christian expressions receive when the messianic possibility has not been accepted. But in this very sacrifice St. Francis lives on. In his work, Francis appears other than Benedict, Bernard or Dominic. The relationship is puzzling, and brings the observer to the danger of misunderstanding it as tragic or protestant. If we look closely, Francis lives on as Christ does in Christian history—the disciple imitating the master. Francis is the author, the founder, the original image— but as a living sacrifice to the master. In every instance those continuing Francis's work can call upon him and so in every instance find not only Francis's but also Christ's face in themselves.

Romano Guardini
in an Afterword to the «Mirror of Perfection»

MAX PICARD

St. Francis of Assisi was completely and totally an exceptional man—exceptional in the immediacy of his love of Christ. With him, one did not find a path to Christ, immediacy had absorbed every path. In Francis, one finds immediacy in itself, absolute immediacy. Only love can be this absolute immediacy. Love, like immediacy, has no genesis, no development and no history; genesis, development and history are all absorbed in the being of love.

Zerstörte und unzerstörbare Welt, 1951
Destroyed and Indestructible World, 1951.

REINHOLD SCHNEIDER

The image of Francis does not live only in the community of his brothers. It lives in homes and fortresses, at markets and among travelers. The visible signs are lost because Francis has entered the very being of people. There, where no eye sees him, he still prepares for the Reign of God. Thoughts, prayers and the spirit in which work is performed all transform themselves under the saint's influence. The power of his interiority, seriousness and joy flow into spiritual reality. This transformation contributes to the tenor of the times and to the current of fate. The saint certainly did not become the Lord of Time: the conflicting powers would have been too strong, too numerous. Yet in him a constellation appeared. It drew glances toward itself and exercised its irresistible influence on human dispositions. And deeds strive toward the direction in which dispositions have turned.

Die Stunde des heiligen Franz von Assisi, 1943
The Hour of St. Francis of Assisi, 1943

I have deluded myself. Without doubt, it was necessary to free the oppressed masses. However, our methods resulted in other oppressions and gruesome massacres. You know I am deathly ill; I feel lost in an ocean of blood formed by countless victims. This was necessary to save our Russia, but it is too late to turn back. We would need ten Francis of Assisis.

Lenin at the end of his life, 1924.

He is the saint who sings, the saint who laughs, the saint who kisses, who plays the violin by bowing a stick on his arm, a dancing angel. He is the saint who joyfully sings to nature, who joyfully loves the nature God has created. He does so not as a pantheist, but clearly in all things, as a gardener loves each flower in his garden for itself. Joy! Joy! It is nothing other than music. He hangs from God on a golden thread, swaying back and forth with life's joy—the troubadour of God. He is inebriated with music and joyful love. Of all the saints, he is the poet; all his deeds are spontaneous rhymes, his words music! And even more than a poetic saint, one would prefer to call him a holy poet.

Heinrich Federer :
Ins Land der Apfelsinen, 1926
Into the Land of Pineapples, 1926

St. Francis walked the world like the Pardon of God. I mean that his appearance marked the moment when men could be recon ciled not only to God but to nature and, most difficult of all, to themselves... He was not only a humanist, especially in the everyday sense of a man who is always humorous, who goes his way and does what no one else would have done... He was the world's once quite sincere democrat.

G. K. Chesterton

From time immemorial the earth has seen both great and glorious persons who have not endeavored to gain praise by individual gargantuan deeds or writing works of poetry or books. These spirits have nonetheless powerfully affected entire peoples and ages. Everyone knew them, spoke of them with enthusiasm and attempted to experience more of them. Their names and reputations were on everyone's lips and throughout the centuries were never lost in the waves and currents of time. Persons so constituted did not derive their effect from individual, separated speeches and works of art. Much more it emanated from the appearance of their whole lives as born of a single, great and individual spirit that all eyes saw as a bright and divine image and example.

H. Hesse Einleitung zu Franz v. Assisi, 1904
Introduction to Francis of Assisi, 1904

We sense that the world situation demands decisive renunciations of consumption. We also sense that we must personalize the redistribution of property and wealth in an attitude of interior freedom from the desire for ownership and power. For such attitudes, there is no better example, other than Jesus of Nazareth, than Francis of Assisi.

Walter Dirks

A savage madman who ran around naked, spoke to animals, gave religious instruction to a wolf and built himself a wife out of snow.

Voltaire 1694-1778

The only perfect Christian since Jesus.

Ernest Renan

My God, give me happiness—not Nietsche's tragic and ferocious happiness, which I do admire, but St. Francis's happiness: a radiating happiness worthy of adoration.

André Gide

The example Francis sets says more to me than a classless society, which can only be the precondition of such an example.

Ludwig Marcuse

The Saint's City

When in Assisi, many believe time has stood still. But the experience is not of a museum dedicated to the preservation of history. Rather, it places people into earlier, distantly believed realities which prove themselves as present, although on a higher level. Until now, I have experienced that impression only in Jerusalem. One does not need fantasy for such an experience because it is not about creating a historical stage with images, but about picking up and putting on the life-filled spirit which flows into every stone, every flower, every corner, every stairway, every church wall and every cry from a bird.

What spirit is that? I find no better answer to that question than the one that Dante gives in canto eleven (Paradiso) of the Divine Comedy. He traces the Umbrian name «Asisum» and the medieval «Ascesi» back to the Latin «ascendere,» to ascend or arise, and sings:

«From it, at that point where the mountainside / grows least abrupt, a sun rose to the world / as this one does at times from Ganges' tide. / Therefore, let no man speaking of that place / call it Ascesi—'I have risen'— but rather, / Oriente—so to speak with proper grace.»

Heinz Malangré, 1985

Going through Assisi means meeting the history and the stories that are bound to Francis.

One can study history but one must track down stories. The city seems almost made for this task with its alleys and corners, archways and taverns, churches and chapels.

There awaits the story of Francis, of him who lived in this city which saw the fateful conflict with his parents; the tales of San Rufino and of the Rocca; the meeting with Clare and the clash between spiritual and temporal powers. There lies the story of his call at San Damiano; of the beginnings which entwine themselves around the Portiuncula; pictures of a man torn between the marketplace and the isolation of the Carceri; the fascination in the Church of St. Clare; stories and ideas that became stone, color and life in the Church of St. Francis. Assisi is all that and more, and such can it become for those who make their way there.

From
«Unterwegs mit Franziskus»
1 (1991) 17

Assisi

There where Francis went he threw
his child's shadow with a burning candle.
There he pulled out his own roots planting
them in the Umbrian wind.
There he gave brothers the gift of poverty
and sowed the seed for birds,
feathered angels. There he renounced
later images—their praise,
their holiness.
There he laid himself
upon the earth
breathed with her, listened to
her stories and told them anew so
that birds and rabbits understood
them as cliffs and water, humans
and trees, the dust under our feet
did as well.

Peter Härtling

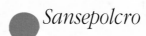
Sansepolcro

Arezzo

Città di Castello

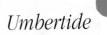
Umbertide

Cortona

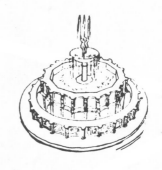
Perugia

Orvieto

Todi

# of Upheaval

LIFE OF ST. FRANCIS	CHURCH HISTORY

LIFE OF ST. FRANCIS

<u>1140</u> Start of construction on the Cathedral of San Rufino in Assisi.

<u>1182</u> John, called Francis, Bernadone born in Assisi.

<u>1198</u> Uprising of the citizens of Assisi against the Staufen fortress above their city.

<u>1202</u> Battle between Assisi and Perugia. Francis imprisoned.

<u>1205</u> Journey to Apulia. Conversion in Spoleto. Pilgrimage to Rome.

<u>1206</u> Encounter with the leper.

<u>1207</u> Renunciation of his paternal inheritance.

<u>1209</u> Close of the conversion story while hearing the Gospel (Mt 10, 7-20) in the Portiuncula on February 24.

<u>1209</u> Letter of Francis to all the faithful.

<u>1210</u> Approval of the Rule by Innocent III.

<u>1212</u> Clare Offreduccio di Favorone joins Francis (March 18). Missionary journey to Syria ends with a shipwreck in Dalmatia.

<u>1214</u> Missionary journey to Morocco ending with illness in Spain.

CHURCH HISTORY

<u>1165</u> Public disputation between the Cathari and Catholic Bishops in Lombres, near Albi.

<u>1179</u> Death of Hildegard von Bingen.

<u>1184</u> Pope Lucius III and Emperor Frederick Barbarossa in Verona. Condemnation of the Cathari and the Waldensians. Bull «Ad abolendam.»

<u>1185-87</u> Pope Urban III resides in Verona.

<u>1187-91</u> Pope Clement III returns to Rome.

<u>1191-98</u> Pope Celestine III.

<u>1198-1216</u> Pope Innocent III.

<u>1198</u> John of Matha founds the Trinitarian Order to ransom imprisoned crusaders.

<u>1206</u> Foundation of the first Dominican Friary in Prouille.

<u>1207</u> Birth of Elizabeth of Hungary.

<u>1209</u> The Patriarch of Jerusalem gives the Hermits of Mt. Carmel their Rule of Life.

SECULAR HISTORY

1217-19 Fifth Crusade (often not counted).

1220-50 Frederick II, Holy Roman Emperor.

1225 Itinerant scholars' songs «Carmina Burana.»

1226-70 Louis IX King of France.

1227 Death of Genghis Kahn.

1228-29 Fifth Crusade (or Sixth).

1229 End of the Albigensian Wars with the Treaty of Paris.
1230 Death of Walther von der Vogelweide.

LIFE OF ST. FRANCIS	CHURCH HISTORY
1215 Meeting with Dominic	1215 Lateran IV. Prohibition of trial by fire.
1216 First Meeting with Hugolin of Ostia.	1216-27 Pope Honorius III.
1217 Pentecost Chapter at the Portiuncula. Division of the Order into Provinces.	1217/18 Birth of St. Bonaventure.
1218 Sermon before the Pope and Cardinals.	
1219 Pentecost Chapter at the Portiuncula. Francis travels to the Near East; arrival in Damietta before August 28. Meeting with the Sultan Melek el Kamil on or about September 26.	
1220 Return to Italy. January 16, protomartyrs in Morocco. Francis with Honorius III in Viterbo. September 22, introduction of the novitiate.	1220 The Augustinian Canon, Ferdinand of Lisbon, later Anthony of Padua, enters the Franciscan Order.
1221 Pentecost Chapter at the Portiuncula. Mission to Germany	
1221 Approval of Third Order Rule.	1222 Death of St. Dominic.
1223 Approval of the final Rule by Honorius III. Francis renounces leadership of the Order. Christmas, manger scene at Greccio.	1223 Servite Order founded.
1224 Mid-September, stigmatization on Mount La Verna. The first Franciscans reach England.	1224 Birth of Thomas of Aquinas.
1225 Summer. Canticle of Brother Sun in San Damiano. Fall. Eye operation in Fonte Colombo.	
1226 Medical treatment in Siena, composition of the «Siena Testament.» Toward the end of September travel to the Portiuncula, where he dies on the evening of October 3. Temporary burial in San Giorgio.	
	1227 Cardinal Hugolin elected pope. As Gregory IX he reigns until 1241.
1228 July 16, canonization in Assisi. The pope lays the corner stone of the new basilica.	
1229 First Life of St. Francis by Thomas of Celano.	1229 The Carmelites come to Europe.
1230 Burial in San Francesco on May 25.	1230 The bull «Quo elongati,» September 28.

The Message

■ ■ ■

Poverty

francis of assisi
a young man
a rich young man
a very rich young man
an only son
of a cloth merchant
a playboy
in assisi
a troubadour

he fell ill
perhaps of riches
who knows
he lived in a time of riches

he fell ill
thus he gains time
he has time
he reflects
he dis-covers—
as columbus america—
he dis-covers
the new testament
the gospel
of jesus of nazareth

francis tries
the gospel
he tries the gospel
on like a skirt
if it fits
if it fits him he
tries out whether
it's okay whether
it sustains
the gospel

he tries whether it's true
he suspects
that it could be true for him
he makes it true
he makes the naked truth true
he makes the true sayings
of the gospel
true

Wilhelm Willms

All the sisters and brothers zealously follow the poverty and humility of Our Lord Jesus Christ. Though rich beyond measure *(II Cor. 8:9)*, He emptied himself for our sake *(Phil. 2:7)* and with the holy virgin, His Mother, Mary, He chose poverty in this world. Let them be mindful that they should have only those goods of this world which, as the Apostle says, "Provide enough food and sufficient clothing; with these we are content" *(I Tim. 6:8)*. Let them particularly beware of money. And let them be happy to live among the outcast and despised, among the poor, the weak, the sick, the uinwanted, the oppressed, and the destitute.

The truly poor in spirit, following the example of the Lord, live in this world as pilgrims and strangers *(Mt. 10:27-29)*. They neither appropriate nor defend anything as their own. So excellent is this most high poverty that it makes us heirs and rulers of the kingdom of heaven. It makes us materially poor, but rich in virtue *(Jn. 2:5)*. Let this poverty alone be our portion because it leads to the land of the living *(Ps 141:6)*. Clinging completely to it let us, for the sake of Our Lord Jesus Christ, never want anything else under heaven.

Rule and Life of the Third
Order Regular, Chapter VI, 21 - 22

Universality

Francis himself took part in the mission of 1219. With a group of brothers he travelled to Syria and Egypt. In Damietta, he came across the army of crusaders—ready for battle. Although the Sultan Melek el Kamil had expressed his readiness for a truce, the papal legate, Pelagius, called for an armed confrontation. Francis joined himself to the side of the princes who wanted to accept the Sultan's offer. He even warned of the grave consequences the battle could have. In fact, one of the most horrible defeats of the Christians ensued.

From Damietta, Francis went to the Sultan, who was favorably inclined toward an Islamic ascetic group, which, at least in externals, was similar to the Franciscans. They called themselves «The Poor» («fakîr» in Arabic, «darvîsh» in Persian) or—after their woolen tunic, «Sufi.» The spiritual preconditions for a friendly meeting of several days were clearly given. Both for the Franciscans, who would often enjoy the hospitality of the Sultan in the future, and for Francis himself the meeting had lasting meaning. After his return, Francis echoed in a series of his own letters a papal document on the Eucharist, a composition that Francis himself may have prompted. In it, one clearly encounters Moslem attitudes and dispositions. Take, for example, the call to render the Incarnation of God and the Eucharist proper adoration. Or take the summons to prostrate oneself on the ground when hearing the name of Jesus.

There are some indications in Arabic literature that Francis had just as much an influence on the Sultan.

A. Rotzetter

BRUDER FRANZ

Meanwhile, while many were joining the brothers, as was said, the most blessed father Francis was making a trip through the Spoleto valley. He came to a certain place near Bevagna where a very great number of birds of various kinds had congregated, namely, doves, crows, and some others popularly called daws. When the most blessed servant of God, Francis, saw them, being a man of very great fervor and great tenderness toward lower and irrational creatures, he left his companions in the road and ran eagerly toward the birds. When he was close enough to them, seeing that they were waiting expectantly for him, he greeted them in his usual way. But, not a little surprised that the birds did not rise in flight, as they usually do, he was filled with great joy and humbly begged them to listen to the word of God. Among the many things he spoke to them were these words that he added: «My brothers, birds, you should praise your Creator very much and always love him; he gave you feathers to clothe you, wings so that you can fly, and whatever else was necessary for you. God made you noble among his creatures, and he gave you a home in the purity of the air; though you neither sow nor reap, he nevertheless protects and governs you without any solicitude on your part.» At these words, as Francis himself used to say and those too who were with him, the birds, rejoicing in a wonderful way according to their nature, began to stretch their necks, extend their wings, open their mouths and gaze at him. And Francis, passing through their midst, went on his way and returned, touching their heads and bodies with his tunic. Finally he blessed them, and then, after he had made the sign of the cross over them, he gave them permission to fly away to some other place. But the blessed father went his way with his companions, rejoicing and giving thanks to God, whom all creatures venerate with humble acknowledgement. (1 Cel 58)

brother wolf
listen
i am a lamb
i know
you are stronger than i
i have no weapon
nothing
other than myself
brother wolf
i am a lamb

i cannot
as wide as you
open my mouth
i cannot bite
cannot dismember
brother wolf
if you want you can eat me

but
brother wolf
be peaceable
do you hear
brother wolf

brother wolf
come
give your paws

do you see
brother wolf

we understand each other
i have something beautiful to say
something gratifying for your stomach

the city of Gubbio
without a doubt
sine dubito

has promised
you brother wolf
every day
as much
as you need to live
so you need not rob
and dismember

W. Willms

And whoever may come to them, friend or foe, thief or robber, they should accept him as a brother.

St. Francis

144

Totally Catholic

All who love the Lord with their whole heart, their whole soul and mind, and with their strength, *(Mt. 12:30)* and love their neighbor as themselves, *(Mt. 22:39)* and who despise the tendency in their humanity to sin, receive the Body and Blood of our Lord Jesus Christ and bring forth from within themselves fruits worthy of true penance;

How happy and blessed are these men and women when they do these things, and persevere in doing them because "the Spirit of the Lord will rest upon them," *(Is. 11:12)* and the Lord will make "His home and dwelling place *(Jn. 14:23)* with them." They are the children of the Heavenly Father *(Mt. 5:45)* whose works they do. They are the spouses, brothers and mothers of Our Lord Jesus Christ *(Mt. 12:50).*

We are his spouses when the faithful soul is united by the Holy Spirit with Our Lord Jesus Christ. We are brothers when we do the will of the Father who is in Heaven *(Mt. 12:50).* We are mothers when we bear Him in our hearts and bodies *(1 Cor. 6:20)* with divine love and with pure and sincere consciences; and we give birth to him through a holy life which should enlighten others because of our example *(Mt. 5:16).*

How glorious it is to have so holy and great a Father in Heaven; and to have such a beautiful and admirable Spouse, the Holy Paraclete; and to have a Brother and Son, so holy, beloved, blessed, humble, peaceful, sweet, lovable and desirable over all things: Our Lord Jesus Christ who gave up his life for his sheep *(Jn. 10:15)* and prayed to the Father, saying: Holy Father, keep in your name *(Jn. 17:11)* those whom you gave me in the world; they are yours and you gave them to me *(Jn. 17:6).* And the word which you gave me I gave to them, and they accepted it and truly believed that it came forth from you. And they have accepted that you sent me *(Jn. 17:8).* I pray for them and not for the world *(Jn. 17:9).* Bless them and sanctify them. I sanctify myself for their sakes, *(Jn. 17:19).* I do not pray only for these but also for those who, through their word, will believe in me *(Jn. 17:20)*; may they be holy in oneness as we are *(Jn. 17:11).* Father, I wish that where I am they too may be and that they may see my glory *(Jn. 17:24)* in your kingdom *(Mt. 20:21).*

St. Francis of Assisi, "Letter to the Faithful". Prologue to the *Rule and Life of the Brothers and Sisters of the Third Order of St. Francis of Assisi,* 1982.

Spirituality

It should be obvious that...(the brothers and sisters) are joyful (Phil. 4:4), goodhumored, and happy in the Lord as they ought to be. And in greeting others, let them say, "The Lord give you peace."
Rule and Life of the Third Order Regular, Chapter V, 20.

It is exciting to know that Third Order men and women religious today, delving back into their origins, now find their basic spirituality as Franciscans expressed in *The Rule and Life of the Brothers and Sisters of the Third Order Regular of St. Francis* approved by Pope John Paul II in 1982. The second Vatican Council had issued the document, *Perfectae Caritatis,* in 1965, addressed to all religious, urging them to return to the gospels and to the original spirit of their founders. Men and women of the Third Order Regular throughout the world, besides following this injunction within their institutes, together engaged in the process of researching their origins and formulated a universally accepted rule. Their goal was to express unity in a common charism in the midst of the diversity of many congregations. After extensive study, dialogue, collaboration, and at times painful sacrifice, they achieved this goal in March 1982 at a meeting in Rome of nearly 200 Superiors General (out of approximately 430) representing 35 countries and nearly 200,000 Franciscan Tertiary Religious. The Brothers and Sisters of the Franciscan Third Order Regular are unique in having accomplished the rewriting of their Rule of Life.

With St. Francis' *Letter to the Faithful* as the prologue, this Rule succinctly states the Third Order charism in Article 2: "...the brothers and sisters of this Order are to persevere in true faith and penance. They wish to live this evangelical conversion of life in a spirit of prayer, of poverty, and of humility."

This *Rule and Life* expresses the Franciscan values: **poverty** - detachment from earthly goods, reverence for all of God's creation and reliance on God's loving providence; **penance** - Biblical *metanoia* which is continuous conversion manifested in works of mercy and charity; **minority** - *minores,* servants of the Word witnessing love and compassion for others; and **contemplation** - "Within themselves, let them always make a dwelling place and home for the Lord God almighty, Father, Son and Holy Spirit so that, with undivided hearts, they may increase in universal love by continually turning to God and to neighbor... and celebrate the Father's love for the world."
Rule and Life, Chapter III, 8-9.

And God inspired me with such faith in his churches that I used to pray with all simplicity saying. "We adore you, Lord Jesus Christ, here and in all your churches in the whole world and we bless you, because by your holy cross you have redeenied the world." The Testament of St. Francis, 1226 (Inserts depict St. Rose of Viterbo ans Bl. Creseentia of Kanfbauerea.)

Contemporary Testimonies

FRANCIS—THE SAINT OF THE MOMENT

St. Francis accompanied me for many years when I worked in a large hospital. I always thought of the story of the brother who called out in the night, «I'm dying! I'm dying of hunger!» Here, as always, was Francis the man of the moment. He did not instruct the brother suffering from fasting who cried out about how fasting pleased God. No, Francis woke the other brothers, and they all ate together. The hungry one had his fill and was not embarrassed, since the others had eaten with him. Francis did what the moment demanded. He cared for the one in need and mobilized the entire community to help.

Retired Hospital Chaplain, 60

Would we accept a man such as St. Francis into our society today? A man who completely confounds our every expectation? A man who lives and deals with others differently than we do? A man who lives in complete poverty and who lives only for God and neighbor? A man who tries to rebuild a house of God that has some cracks? Would we accept such a man? Would we join with him so as to follow after Christ?

Student, 15

It is Francis's unshakable faith and the resolute endeavor to be an instrument of peace that impresses me. The consistency with which the saint gave up all his material riches, realized his aspirations for true riches and turned himself into the ideal of the Sermon on the Mount in his love of neighbor, makes the gospel more meaningful for me. It prevents me from regarding it as unattainable.

St. Francis's Canticle of Brother Sun, written in the greatest pain, challenges me to seek and praise God in all of His creation. As the three young men in the furnace once invited all the elements to the praise of the creator, Francis glorifies the creator and ruler of all things in every element and creature. He thus reminds us not only of our responsibility to nature, but also invites us to go through the world with open eyes, experiencing God in the mysteries of his creation. This message, and Francis's invariable faith in God, serve as a model and foothold to help me live my own faith better.

Student, 15

«Farewell, Mount La Verna; farewell, Brother Falcon.» So said St. Francis as he withdrew from the place of his stigmatization. Two years remained to him—two years of illness and pain. From then on, he had to let himself be carried wherever he went. During this time he created the «Canticle of Brother Sun»!

Today Brother Wolf and Brother Falcon disappear, trees and flowers have become as unhealthy as water and fish. Today the «Canticle of Brother Sun,» my sisters and brothers, may comfort us. It expresses what had not yet come to light at the beginning of the thirteenth century.

Neither the big bang nor global warming make brothers and sisters for us out of the landscapes and animals whose disappearance we mourn, but rather a common creation and a common death.

For this reason we should also praise the Lord through our Sister, Earthly Time. She leads onward, experienced differently by each created being. She passes on and makes others pass on; she herself cannot create. To her, God entrusted his secret thoughts and creative word. In her, everything He designed becomes tested and woven before His all-seeing eyes. Only at the end of time, when every mortal creature will have praised him and the tapestry of creation hangs complete, will we recognize the completeness of its eternal beauty.

Journalist, 57

In my experience, contemporary persons perceive Francis merely as a far-off mythological figure or a man demanding the impossible—that we distance ourselves from our consumption. Many regard this demand as unrealizable and risky—understandable in an age stamped with power and appearance. For me, Francis possesses a meaning greater than we are willing to accept. With God's help he stood firm against a flood of antipathy and misunderstanding. He did not see his purpose fulfilled in power and authority, but through service of God and humanity became a bit closer to God's Kingdom. Francis asked himself what vocation God had given him. He found it in serving his neighbors and renouncing the unnecessary. Eventually, those who do not feel called to a particular mission turn to hate and violence. This is as true today as it was in Francis's time. One need only look at the readiness of those whose dreams end in frustration to become violent.

Student, 16

Discourse about faith forms a necessary part of life and leads to life. Passing on faith becomes part of the whole of life.

Regarding Francis, these remarks mean that he did not lead the isolated life of an ideological icon. He related to the whole of humankind—particularly the poor—and to the whole of creation.

The story of his life helps us pause to reflect upon our own situation. We too can learn to see with different eyes and another soul. We too may have a chance to see anew the greatness of God which gives even the smallest creature air, light and life itself, that it might breathe and rejoice in its being.

Educators, particularly those working with children, where the opportunity is greatest, should keep an eye open for settings where the small show greatness, the few mean a great deal and the simple become many sided.

Can we not then awaken to a lasting satisfaction. . . the precondition of peace?

Housewife, 38

For the sake of Christ, Francis became fanatical for poverty.

The majority of Brazil is damned to poverty. Following the Saint of Assisi, the Brazilian Church has obligated itself to be available to the poor and to stand up for their rights.

In this battle, the sons and daughters of St. Francis fill the front ranks.

Bishop, 78

MY GOD, I LOVE YOU BOUNDLESSLY. MY COMPLETE FIDELITY AND ALL MY THOUGHTS BELONG TO YOU IN EVERY MOMENT.

This motto stands at the head of two works of music and poetry about St. Francis by the artist Karl Hagen von Horix.

I turned sixty-five years old in April of this year. As I think back many years, years which are like yesterday to me, I see myself, among many other places, at Castle Zeil in July of 1950, a guest of Prince Alois Loewenstein, then president of the central committee of German Catholics. My father, the composer Karl Hagen von Horix, was performing his two works, «The Legend of St. Francis of Assisi» and «Evening on Mount La Verna.» I read the texts and joined him at the piano. The curious atmosphere I remember well; it had not appeared at any of our many concerts between 1947 and 1952. Some of the invited guests, among them the grandson of the Austo-Hungarian Emperor, Otto von Hapsburg, independently of each other, said they had seen the appearance of a capuche around my head as I read about the death of St. Francis. I myself had the indescribable feeling of being carried quite close to the saint. Since then, St. Francis has never let me go. He has accompanied me throughout my life—the years of musical and theological study, as a lay minister in the Church, as a teacher in adult education programs and now, as housewife and mother.

Francis is neither merely a saint of the middle ages, nor simply a comforting companion during the difficult times of World War II. He is also a man of today: spokesperson for the poor, the suffering, the endangered environment and the defenseless creature. He is a saint of the moment, one who both greets others with «Pax et Bonum,» (Peace and All Good) and lives accordingly.

When we gave concerts, one reporter once described me as «St. Francis's virgin sister, Clare.» What more could I wish for, than—at least in the mind of a journalist—to be the sister of the Poverello, of the «Herald of the Great King,» as Francis described himself. While such a thought, even in the remotest corner of one's mind, is presumptuous, it remains a pearl in the parched and glowing sand of life.

Author, 65

What does Francis mean to me?

I marvel at Francis. He managed to do what is so very neces sary today—loving and sharing from one's own costs. He did not renounce the superfluous by being patronizing, but shared his reality and his existence. Francis, the son of rich parents, spoiled, covetous and egotistical, did not merely question his own life, he turned it topsy-turvy. Why so suddenly? What must he have experienced to act in such a manner? What sort of power and love must have moved and claimed him? Despite people's shock, the sadness and anger of his parents, Francis held fast to his decision to give his life to God among the poor and the sick, humans and animals. And he did so throughout his whole life, not only until the moment he realized what such dedication involved.

I envy Francis and long for such an emotion and deep love, for such a closeness to God that works such wonders.

Student, 24

Francis was young, successful, gifted, from a good home, had good connections and a sure career. According to society, he lived a dream come true. And yet precisely in the midst of this comfort and ease—one thinks of one's own situation—Francis sought a way to God, to Christ.

He did not preach that others must «accept» the will of God in their fate («acceptance» has, thanks to its constant repetition, become such a trite word). No, Francis sought God's will in scripture and prayer and then proceeded to fulfill it—naive, without self-absorbed doubts about the authenticity and veracity of scripture. For Francis, one, meaning the other, was not to follow Christ. He himself followed Christ, even if it meant failure in leading his own order or in the collapse of «Brother Ass,» his own body.

The bitter becoming sweet describes his conversion and illumination. For the author of the «Canticle of Brother Sun,» words were too weak, too incomplete to express how God had converted him.

Assisi! Umbria! There I found the spirit of St. Francis pre sent and alive. It scratched at my hubris and gave me hope that the camel might yet pass through the needle's eye. I have also found this spirit in some of Francis's brothers today, in those who seek to build themselves up in the service of others. They do so, like Francis, not because they lack recognition, success or ability, but because they are exemplary, strong persons.

Physician, 53

Mario von Galli's book on St. Francis came as a serendipitous gift and awakened my strong interest in the Poverello. I recall my first visit to Assisi, the Basilica of St. Francis and the tomb. Hundreds of people pushed each other, each exuding the sweat of summer. There were Japanese with their cameras, Americans with caps and young people in the fashionably poor look of St. Francis, each wearing a wooden tau-cross around his or her neck. The crowd took me along until we finally got a view of the grave which looked like a stone tower wrapped in metal bands. «Those are bands around my heart—broken by great pain.» Words from one of Grimm's Fairy Tales rose in my heart as I automati cally genuflected and found a seat in the small wooden pew. I knelt, looked and felt what lay behind human existence. I felt it and knew it as I later found myself with a wet face behind a pil lar in the lower church.

Housewife, 53

When I was fourteen years old, my tonsils were removed and I spent a week in the hospital. My Godmother, an Aachen Franciscan, was stationed there. She brought me a biography of St. Francis (by Jörgensen?), which I read quite eagerly. I lay alone and undisturbed in my room. In the evenings, she would come to visit and I could ask her questions.

Most frequently and persistently, I found myself impressed with St. Francis's cry, «Love is not being lived!» It occurred to me that God loves us—simply loves us without our having earned it and without demands. How horrible it is that so few, including myself, love him in return! No, I thought, that cannot be. I wanted to do all I could to give a loving answer to his love.

The most radical answer seemed to me religious life, and I could not rest until I had said «yes.» After my training as a kindergarten teacher, I worked for a year until I turned twenty-one (then the legal age of majority) and became a Franciscan— against my parents' wishes. Today, some thirty years later, they have forgiven me for this step.

During a pilgrimage to Assisi in 1988, another phrase of St. Francis became important for me. He said to his brothers, «I have done what is mine to do; may the Lord show you what is yours to do,» as he lay on his deathbed.

So did he point to his source and his goal; he encouraged each of his brothers and sisters to seek and answer God—with the answer of love.

Religious Sister, 51

I had my first encounter with St. Francis while I was still a child. Our parish had put on a play about him. At the time, two things especially impressed me, and they have marked my thoughts about Francis ever since. I marveled at the Francis who one day changed himself from a rich, arrogant youth into a simple, undemanding man—and who readily and thankfully gave back his life to God at his end (Sister Death). The celebrations around Francis in 1993 constantly impel me, in the midst of an egocentric and consumption-oriented society, to learn once again how to live life simply, to be open to others, to rejoice in creation and help to preserve it.

Teacher, 62

Francis, please excuse me, but I have to say this. You don't exactly make it easy for someone to live a «Franciscan» life! Who can live today as you once lived? Your existence was so immediate and so consistent, and yet so free, full of lightness and life! You were, at the same time, completely devoted to God, your fellows and the Church! You were so completely «without»: without fear, compartmentalization, prejudice, second thoughts, privileges, security, defenses or masks. Why, we could be injured! One lovely day we would run around with open wounds—as you did at the end. And so I ask, who can live today as you once lived? (Or, more honestly, who wants to? A slightly simpler life is fine, but who wants to be really poor?)

You know, I've often thought that we Franciscans would have it a lot easier if we clearly distanced ourselves from you. We should calmly admit that we want to grasp only one or another of your stimuli. Even with that, we'd have enough to do without always having to awaken these dangerous reminders of you because of our name.

It's amazing that you, a medieval man, still can always make me so restless. It seems that even today you can suddenly tap me on the shoulder as I walk along the alleyways of Assisi! Your sting is still strong—even after eight hundred years!

Franciscan, 32

Throughout his life, Francis wrote «joy» in capital letters.

Think of his youth, of the many feasts he spent with his friends. Even so, at one point this joy began to stick in his craw.

Yet, even as he turned away from this dissolute life, he did not leave joy behind. On the contrary, in his modesty, simplicity and freedom from the demands of society he found true joy—and many friends besides.

Francis's life shows me that I all too often blind myself to the obvious. I rejoice when others recognize my accomplishments, but … I rejoice when someone compliments me, but … I often rejoice, but.… The simple joys, which come from God, I overlook much too easily.

Student, 24

In Francis, I see the universal religious person, the one we so urgently need as a model today. He discovered a way of life for himself and his brothers. While radical, it is neither brutal nor hard; it takes the gospel at its word without the inflexibility of fundamentalism and it accepts the asceticism of self-imposed limits without becoming unyielding, bitter and uncreative. Asceticism is poetic and affirms the world. Maintaining a proper balance, so that life does not envelop itself in extremes or hardness, is typical for the Franciscan person. The lifestyle that Francis created and sanctified for Christianity, the life of a itinerant mendicant, contains all this. Is there any lifestyle for us today that more sincerely speaks to our needs and longings? Look at the signs of our times: on the one hand we see the forced movement beyond borders (refugees, those looking for political asylum and immigrants); on the other hand we find voluntary movement everywhere (educational travel, tourism and our insatiable, never before experienced mobility).

Author, 44

The saint who loves animals fascinates me. I became more familiar with him and was lucky enough to visit his home of Umbria. There I discovered a world in which strictness was not all that strict, in which fantasy and joy belong to the richness of the essential.

«Brother Sun, Sister Moon, Sister Spider, Brother Wolf» were not romantic sayings. This was a language I could understand, the brilliant expression of the tremendous unity of creation. In the world of Franciscan thought, I found a world in which I could breathe. I now allowed the other saints their sanctity— each in his or her own way. In the same spirit I believe that God can rejoice over my timorous little light in the midst of the crowd of his saints. Here I can trust that he also hears my song, just as he heard violin music when Francis «played» branches and twigs. Here suffering can be released, withstood and blossom into a new life which increases the amount of love in the world and allows divine joy to stream out of all things.

Editor, 56

Francis of Assisi embodies the eternal hope of humankind for a better future. He communicates values and truths which are valid for our time and exist for all time. They arise from a fundamental credibility that touches our most profound depths. His spirituality shows us a point of departure and method for self-discovery and offers the possibility of unity between persons and all of creation. Francis of Assisi is a man and a saint whose faith and love can always reorient one on the path to true humanity.

Painter, 55

Pope Innocent III led the medieval papacy and Church to the heights of their power. Francis was his contemporary; in him God pointed his finger at the Church and its hierarchy, and continues to do so. The saint has impressed me throughout my whole life. He amazes me as a man, a companion to his brothers and a Christian symbol. Yet I ask myself if I pay too little attention to the first three decades of his life. I wonder how much and in what sense these years are a precondition for a Franciscan life.

Teacher, 62

Francis's close connection to animals, the world and the stars has always pleased me.

He may have been simple, and yet his spirit lives even today.

In the meantime, science has confirmed his view of reality: the stars, human beings, animals and plants all consist of the same atomic building blocks.

Even the stars are our brothers and sisters!

Sculptor, 47

THE SAINTS

Catherine Labouré

The Chapel
of the Apparitions Today

"Is this the Holy Chapel?" asks a visitor to the Chapel of the Apparitions.

This chapel is indeed a holy place. All those who enter it are immediately struck by the pervading atmosphere of peace and serenity. Those who come have no doubt as to the source of this atmosphere. As a young student commented, *"She came here once, and she is still here."*

The quiet of the chapel strikes visitors whether they are tourists or pilgrims. Tourists who are led to this site

Yesterday and today

by a few obscure lines in their guidebooks at first take pictures, and speak loudly, just as if they were visiting any other tourist site. Yet, they quickly lower their voices as they try to understand what is different about this place.

The pilgrim, especially if he or she is visiting the chapel for the first time, cannot help but notice the welcoming expression of the statue of the Virgin of Radiant Graces. The words of Mary to Catherine Laboure are a heartfelt invitation: *"Come to the foot of this altar. Here graces will be showered on all those who ask for them with ardent faith."* Visitors come and kneel on the steps of the altar where, close to Mary and her son Jesus who is present in the tabernacle, they express their concerns, joys, sorrows, petitions, and gratitude.

Just like the woman in the Gospel who tried to just touch Jesus's cloak in order to be healed, many pilgrims express their faith and prayers in simple ways. For many, offering flowers expresses what they are unable to say with words. A young man asked for example, *"What color flowers would best express my gratitude to the Blessed Virgin?"* A little later he returned with a bouquet of red roses. Sometimes, a young bride will come with her bridegroom to place her wedding bouquet at Mary's feet. Often, the offering is more modest: a simple little bouquet placed in thanksgiving by a woman at the site of Mary's apparitions. Or, it may be a few flowers timidly laid down by a man who wants to express to Mary his gratitude for *"the confession which has set me free."*

Other pilgrims express their prayers in writing on small pieces of paper. This little scrap of paper is then placed in a wicker basket in the sanctuary, and thus becomes the prayer of the entire community. These petitions are anonymous prayers shared with Mary who welcomes our anxiety, fear, and discouragement with as much love as she welcomes our trust, thanksgiving, and joy.

158

"On December 8th, I was at my daughter's school sorting clothes for the poor. The woman working with me told me that she was stopping to go to Mass. Since I did not want to stay behind alone, I joined her. I had long-abandoned any religious practice. When I entered the brilliantly-lit chapel and saw a large crowd of people praying and singing, I was astonished. A profound but difficult to describe feeling overcame me. When I heard the priest say the words, "Happy are those who are invited to the Lord's supper," I felt as if this was a personal invitation that Christ was addressing to me. Without knowing quite why, I went to communion. This encounter with Jesus was an unforgettable experience of grace in my life.

The next day, I returned on my own to the chapel. I thanked Mary fervently. I asked her to help me to know and love her Son more intimately. Thanks to a friend, I became aware of the Catholic Theological Institute of Paris where I have often taken courses. The Eucharist has become an indispensable part of my life. I hunger for Jesus. Through Mary I have dedicated my life to him. It was not long before my daughter told me: 'Mother, you are not the same. You are more patient than you once were. You are always so attentive to the needs of others.' Yes, truly my life has changed."

———————

"I have been very sick. I have come to implore you Virgin Mary to pray for me. Please help me to deal with my alcoholism."

"Holy Virgin Mary, you know me well. I have come to thank you for being my Mother... and to also ask you to pray for my family, my husband, and the baby I am carrying."

"Virgin Mary, I prayed asking you to help my nephew, Michael, find work. Not only has he found a job, but he also escaped injury in a serious car accident. I will spend the rest of my days thanking you along with all those who come to pray in this luminous Chapel."

"Mary, I am praying for the parents of Jennifer (age 4) and Emily (age 18 months). They were both killed in a car accident. I also pray for all those who are cold and hungry."

"Lord, I ask you to sustain my faith as I prepare to be baptized."

"Mary, I confide to your care a young drug addict that I know. He only thinks of death. Please give him the Mother's love he has never known. Aid all the young who are searching for love in their lives."

Very often, great personal suffering is the subject of the prayers left in the basket. One mother left her prayer intention for her infant son suffering from pneumonia: *"After visiting here and presenting my request to Mary, my suffering is the same, but now I am not carrying it alone, Mary is carrying it with me."*

The prayers of the pilgrims to Mary and to Catherine lead them to the Eucharist. Each day there are three masses offered at the shrine. These celebrations underline the Eucharistic character of the Chapel of the Apparitions. Each afternoon there is also Marian prayer offered, usually the rosary. These devotions conclude with the Benediction of the Blessed Sacrament.

Each day numerous pilgrims visit the Chapel of the Apparitions. During the winter an average of 2,500 come, with over 4,000 visiting each day during the summer. They come from Paris and its suburbs, from all over France, Europe, and the five continents of the world.

Some come as part of a parish, diocesan, or national pilgrimage. Others belong to a particular movement in the Church. Others come with their families or friends, some come by themselves.

If most of the pilgrims are Catholics, there are also those who are unbelievers, some who are Orthodox, Protestants, and sometimes even Muslims and Buddhists.

Those who come are of all ages, from new-born infants brought by their mothers directly from the hospital, to a 90 year old grandmother who supported by her cane comes to make a little pilgrimage. Young and old, children, students, fathers, mothers, single adults, young husbands and wives, all have something to say to Mary. They all seek a share of the interior peace that she radiates.

Some visitors only stay long enough to say a short prayer. Others stay for Mass or to recite the Rosary. Many return time and time again; they know that Mary always awaits them.

Many pilgrims want to know what took place in this chapel to account for its atmosphere. In a nearby room the sisters feature a video presentation which explains the story of Catherine Laboure, the apparitions, and the message of the Miraculous Medal. Several Daughters of Charity from the motherhouse community are always available to assist pilgrims and answer their questions.

The purchase of medals is often the occasion for conversations between the pilgrims and the sisters who staff the gift shop. Visitors often spontaneously take the sisters into their confidence. A young German musician received a medal from one

"I return again, ashamed but determined to ask for what I need to sustain the life that has been given me by your Son. Life is a precious gift and should consist of more than mere survival... I have nothing. I have lost everything. I am hungry, but a disability keeps me from working. I do not want to be reduced to begging on the street. Please, provide for what I need... I look to you with my hands outstretched to receive what you will give me. I know that you receive countless requests, but please hear my urgent plea. Please help me. I am counting on you."

"I come today at a time of great distress in my life to appeal to your goodness. I hope that this cry of love which comes from the depths of my heart will touch you sincerely. My father will soon be 56 years old. I beseech you not to abandon him to the terrible cancer that he is suffering. He is too young to die. I love him more than anyone else in this world. Help him to return to health. There is not much time. I ask you to act quickly. Thank you with all my heart."

VENEZ AU PIED DE CET AUTEL LA LES GRACES SERONT REPANDUES SUR TOUS

...CROIS ET CONFESSE VOTRE SAINTE ET IMMACULÉE CONCEP...

O MARIE CONÇUE SANS PÉCHÉ PRIEZ POUR NOUS QUI AVONS RECOURS A VOUS

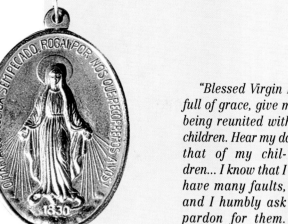

of his friends. His friend told him to go to the chapel "where extraordinary things happen!" He visited the chapel and returns frequently. He told one of the sisters, *"Believe me sister, over the last two years my life has changed."* He now tells his musician friends about the message of the Miraculous Medal.

An elderly woman told the sisters: *"I would like to buy a Miraculous Medal for each of my 18 grandchildren. This will be their inheritance from their grandmother."*

When buying a medal, a woman named Nadine told the sisters about her brother's illness. The sisters promised to pray for him. She returned three months later: *"I bought a medal hoping that it would help cure my brother Eric, and I know that you prayed for him. My brother was not healed. God called him to himself, but he left this world in peace and he was reconciled to God. We prayed for the healing of his body, and Mary through her Son, obtained healing for his soul. Today, I have returned to thank her for this."*

These are the miracles performed at the chapel. Mary continues the redemptive work of her Son.

There is nothing beautiful about the little alleyway that connects the street to the chapel. However, this area plays an important role in helping the visitor and pilgrim to leave behind the noise and busyness of the world and prepare themselves for the quiet of the sanctuary. A series of bas-relief sculptures on the walls relate the story of the Chapel. In this entranceway, sisters and pilgrims meet formally and informally. Pilgrims can ask to speak with a priest, or request that Mass be offered for their particular intentions.

All this activity often intrigues passers-by. Many enter to see for themselves what is going on. Often they are responding unconsciously to the same invitation issued by the Lord to the first disciples:

"Come and see."

"Blessed Virgin Mary, you are full of grace, give me the grace of being reunited with my wife and children. Hear my daily prayer and that of my children... I know that I have many faults, and I humbly ask pardon for them. Reunite us I pray, so that we can together love you from our hearts."

"God alone knows how many people I see praying fervently about so many problems... When I see them I offer a prayer asking for their prayers to be answered, if it is God's will.

Isn't this what the Communion of Saints is all about?"

"As I passed by on the street I did not know what was going on inside. I was intrigued by the great crowds of people coming and going through the doors. Overcome by curiosity, I entered as well. I followed the crowd and arrived at the Chapel...

I was surprised to see everyone being so quiet, in contrast to the noise on the street. I sat down to rest for a moment. Mass was being celebrated.

The "Our Father" was being recited. I recognized the prayer that my grandmother had taught me so long ago, and which for such a long time I had forgotten.

I was very touched, and have returned to the Chapel many times since. Mary led me to talk to a priest to recover peace for my conscience, and my Faith...

I recount these events to encourage others to explore the entranceway which leads to the Chapel, to Mary, and to Jesus."

Catherine Labouré

"O Mary, conceived without sin, pray for us who have recourse to you"
Even before the definition of the dogma of the Immaculate Conception by Pope Pius IX in 1854, this short prayer was made known to the world through the Miraculous Medal. Mary chose to reveal this message to a 24 year old village girl who was preparing to become a Daughter of Charity.

Biography

From her infancy, Catherine had a great devotion to Mary. Born on May 2, 1806, in the town of Fain-les-Moutiers, Catherine was the eighth child of her family. Her mother worn out by seventeen pregnancies (with ten surviving children), and the rigors of farm life, died prematurely on October 9, 1815. Catherine grew up in a family in which prayer was a part of daily life. While the adults were gathered around her dying mother, Catherine climbed on a chair and took the family's statue of Our Lady in her arms. Timidly, but with conviction, she asked Mary to take the place of her mother. Her tears stopped and she returned to her mother's deathbed certain that she would not have to face life alone.

After his wife's burial, Pierre Labouré agreed to his sister's suggestion that she care for his two youngest children, Catherine (age 9) and Tonine (age 7). The two girls went to live with their cousins at Saint Remy, a village which was 9 kilometers from their home. Marie-Louise, the eldest daughter, took over her mother's place in running the family and the farm.

After two years Mr. Labouré, who missed his two daughters, arranged for their return. The children were thrilled to be home. Catherine in particular was overjoyed to be reunited with her father. She also developed a close bond with her little brother Auguste, (age 9) who had been disabled in a carriage accident. Her chores included taking care of the farm's 600 doves.

The Labouré farm

Marie-Louise taught her younger sister to work in the stable, the garden, how to clean house, and how to cook. Catherine worked diligently at all these tasks. When Marie-Louise announced that she was going to fulfill her dream of entering the Daughters of Charity, Catherine told her sister Tonine, "The two of us will run the house!"

Catherine entered into her new family responsibilities. The first to rise, she carefully attended to all her chores. She cooked, took care of the cows, collected eggs, made bread, took care of the doves, and did the wash.

On January 25, 1818, Catherine made her First Communion. With great devotion, she often attended daily mass in the town of Moutiers-Saint-Jean which was four kilometers from her village. Tonine was upset, thinking that her sister was taking on more than her strength would allow. She also noticed that Catherine fasted on Fridays and Saturdays. Tonine thought that Catherine was too young to undertake these practices, and she threatened to tell their father. Catherine who possessed a strong character did not relent.

A vocation opposed

One night, Catherine had a dream. In her village church an elderly priest was saying Mass. The priest gazed at Catherine and said to her: *"My daughter, you may flee me now, but one day you will be happy to come to me. Do not forget that God has plans for you."* Several years later when Catherine visited the Daughters of Charity at Chatillon-sur-Seine, she noticed a painting on the parlor wall. She was shocked to recognize the priest in the painting as the priest she had seen in her dream. She asked, *"Who is this priest?"* A sister told her that it was Saint Vincent de Paul.

When she was eighteen, Catherine finally received her father's permission to go to Chatillon to live with a cousin who ran a little finishing school. She wanted to learn how to read and write. These were prerequisites for joining the Daughters of Charity. The other young women looked down on Catherine because of her country ways. She lost her confidence and returned to the family farm. She had only learned to sign her name and write a few words.

God's call was pressing. She wondered how she should tell her father of her desire to become a Daughter of Charity. Catherine knew that he would oppose such an idea. He felt that by sacrificing his daughter Marie-Louise he had already given enough. Catherine patiently waited until she was of legal age. Even then her father refused to give his permission. He felt Catherine was too useful on the farm, and that her hard work, and happy temperament would make her a perfect farmer's wife and a wonderful mother. Mr. Laboure even tried to find her a husband. He was wasting his time. Catherine remained faithful to God's call.

The dovecote

Mr. Laboure knew that since his daughter had his temperament, it would be difficult to change her mind. He therefore tried another approach. Catherine was sent to Paris to help her brother Charles run his small restaurant. Charles's wife had died, and he was in need of assistance. Obediently, Catherine left for the city still hurting from her father's refusal. Her abilities as a cook and a housekeeper attracted numerous suitors, but Catherine remained aloof from them all. Charles understood his sister's unhappiness. When he remarried on February 3, 1829 he agreed that she could leave. Instead of returning home, Catherine wrote to her sister Marie-Louise who advised her to go to Chatillon to stay with her older brother Hubert who had married their cousin who ran the finishing school.

"You should spend some time with our dear sister–in–law in order to get a little education. This will be help-ful to you whatever you may do. You need to learn how to speak better French, how to write, do figures, and above all learn piety, fervor, and love of the poor."

Catherine, who was always uncomfortable around the city girls, spent more and more time with the local

Pierre Laboure, Catherine's father

Madeleine Gontard, Catherine's mother

Daughters of Charity. Hubert spoke to his father on his sister's behalf. Pierre Laboure finally gave in before the unmistakable signs that his daughter had a vocation. On January 22, 1830, Catherine began her postulancy at Chatillon.

The Apparitions

On Wednesday, April 21, 1830, Catherine entered the novitiate of the Daughters of Charity located at their motherhouse in Paris. Catherine's spiritual experiences during this time would be extraordinary. She would tell her confessor about everything that was happening to her. At first he paid no attention.

On Sunday, April 25, a few days after her arrival, Catherine joined the other sisters in celebrating the Translation of the Relics of Saint

Seminary Sisters

The church of Fain-les-Moutiers

Vincent de Paul. During the revolutionary period these relics had been hidden for safekeeping. The Archbishop of Paris now wished to honor the saint whom everyone recognized as "the father of the poor." He hoped that this celebration would rekindle the faith of the residents of the capital. An immense procession wound through the streets of Paris from Notre Dame Cathedral to the chapel of the priests of the Congregation of the Mission at 95 rue de Sèvres.

When Catherine returned to the motherhouse after the celebration she had a vision of Saint Vincent's heart. This apparition was repeated for three successive days. Each time the color of the heart changed. At first it was white, symbolizing peace, then it was red symbolizing love, and then it was black symbolizing misfortune.

"Every time that I returned from Saint Lazare, I would go to our chapel where above the little reliquary containing Saint Vincent's relics his heart would appear to me. This happened three days in a row.

The first day the heart was white symbolizing peace, calm, innocence, and union.

On the second day it appeared to be red like the charity which must enflame our hearts. I sensed that the Community would undergo renewal and would spread throughout the world.

Finally, on the last day it was black. This distressed me greatly. I do not know why, nor do I know if this sadness was related to the revolution that would soon take place. I spoke to

my confessor who tried to calm me as much as possible, and distract me from all these thoughts."

In her daily life there was nothing that distinguished Catherine from the other young sisters. Their day began at 4:00 a.m. After Mass, the directress would give a conference on the vocation of the Daughters of Charity to serve the poor. She also gave them instructions about prayer and its role in the life of a Daughter of Charity. She spoke of the importance of the Eucharist. Catherine kept hidden the great favor that she had been granted: seeing our Lord in the Blessed Sacrament. On the feast of the Holy Trinity she also had a vision of Christ the King.

"I was also favored with another great grace, that of seeing Our Lord in the Blessed Sacrament. This happened throughout my time in the novitiate until I allowed myself to doubt. After this I saw nothing because I had doubted this profound mystery, and I believed that I may have been mistaken in what I had seen."

The days passed peacefully. Catherine, who had desired to see Mary since her childhood prayed fervently to be granted this favor. On July 18, Sister Martha the novice directress spoke about Saint Vincent's devotion to the

Blessed Mother. That evening when Catherine went to bed she had a feeling that she would see Mary that night. This apparition took place at 11:30 that evening. She would tell her confessor about this experience. Later he asked her to put her recollections in writing. These precious remembrances survive.

"At 11:30 in the evening I heard someone calling me: 'Sister, Sister, Sister.' I awoke and looked in the direction that I heard the voice coming from. I saw a little child dressed in white who appeared to be about 4 or 5 years old. The child said to me: 'Let us go to the Chapel. Get up quickly and go to the chapel. The Blessed Virgin is waiting for you.' The thought came to me: 'but someone will hear me.' The child told me: 'Do not worry, it is 11:30 in the evening and everyone is asleep. Come, I am waiting for you.'

I arose and dressed quickly while the child waited for me at the foot of the bed. He followed me, or rather I followed him. He was always on my left. He shone brightly and illuminated the path we were taking. This astonished me greatly. But I was even more surprised as I entered the chapel and found that the door opened at the child's touch. My amazement was made complete when I saw that all the candles and lights in the chapel were illuminated as if for midnight mass. I did not yet see the Blessed Virgin. The child led me into the sanctuary to the chair where the sisters' director always sat. I fell to my knees, and the child remained with me. I thought a long time

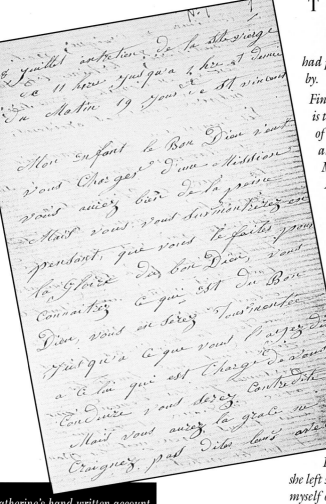

Catherine's hand-written account
of the apparition of July 18

had passed, and looked to see if the sisters on the night watch passed by.

Finally, the time had come. The child sensed this and told me: 'Here is the Blessed Virgin. She is here.' I heard a rustlingly like the sound of a silk dress. This sound was coming from the Gospel side of the altar... I doubted at first that this was the Blessed Virgin. Meanwhile, the child said to me: 'Here is the Blessed Virgin.' After this, it was impossible for me to describe what I was feeling or what was going on around me. It seemed that I still could not recognize the Blessed Virgin... Now the child no longer spoke to me in a child's voice but in a man's strong voice.

Then I recognized the Blessed Virgin, I quickly knelt before her on the steps of the altar and put my hand on her knees. Then, I spent the greatest moments of my life. It would be impossible for me to describe how I felt. She told me how I must conduct myself during the struggles that would come to me in the future. She pointed to the foot of the altar with her left hand and said that it was there I was to open my heart, there I would receive all the consolation that I needed... There I should ask for the explanation of all the things that I had seen. Oh! She explained everything to me!...

I do not know how long I stayed there. All I know is that when she left she suddenly was gone in the same way that she arrived. I found myself on the steps of the altar and I saw that the child was where I had last seen him. He told me, 'She is gone.' We returned the same way we had come with the path illumined before us. The child was always on my left. I believe that this child was my guardian angel who had become visible to guide me to the Blessed Virgin. Because I had prayed so hard he obtained this grace for me. He was dressed in white, and was miraculously illuminated. He seemed to be about 4 or 5 years old.

I returned to my bed. I heard the clock sound the time. It was 2:00 a.m. I could not get back to sleep."

In the course of their long conversation, Mary told Catherine that she would be given a mission. Like all God's messengers, she could expect to encounter numerous difficulties and suffer many contradictions. In an account written on October 30, 1876, Catherine reported some of Mary's words.

"My child, God wants to give you a mission. You will encounter many difficulties but you will be able to overcome them if you do everything for God's glory. You must believe that all this comes from God, and you will not be at peace until you tell your confessor about what has happened. You will encounter obstacles, but you will be given the grace that you need. Do not fear. You will see certain things. Tell what you will see. You will be inspired in your prayers."

"The times are very evil. Misfortunes afflict France,... the entire world will experience misfortunes of all sorts... The moment will come when the danger will be great. People will believe that all is lost... The cross will be scorned, blood will flow in the streets, the entire world will be saddened... But come to the foot of this altar, there

abundant graces will be spread over all those who ask for them with confidence and fervor. They will be given to the great and the small..."

Then Catherine recalled the message that Mary told her to give to her confessor Father Jean-Marie Aladel:

"The Blessed Virgin would like you to begin an organization. You will be its founder and director. This will be the Association of the Children of Mary. The Blessed Virgin will give you many graces..."

Catherine's life continued tranquilly. However, during the last days of July a revolution broke out in Paris which overthrew the king of France, Charles X. Her confessor, Father Aladel was astonished. His penitent had predicted this would happen. He wondered whether Catherine's accounts could be authentic and not the product of her imagination as he originally had thought. This question was reinforced when she later told him of a new apparition of Mary.

Over the years Catherine wrote several accounts of this second apparition.

"On November 27, 1830, which was the Saturday before the first Sunday of Advent, at 5:30 in the evening after meditation and during the Grand Silence... I seemed to hear a sound of rustling silk coming from the side of the tribune near the painting of Saint Joseph. Looking in that direction I saw the Blessed Virgin.

The Blessed Virgin was dressed in white in a robe of silk..., she wore a long white veil. Under her veil I saw that her hair was covered. The figure was standing. Her feet were resting on a globe, or better on what appeared to me to be a half of a globe. She had her hands raised gracefully, and her eyes were elevated to heaven. Her face was quite beautiful. I cannot describe it.

Suddenly, I noticed that her fingers each had rings covered with beautiful stones, some were small and some were large. These stones emitted rays of light, each more beautiful than the next. The

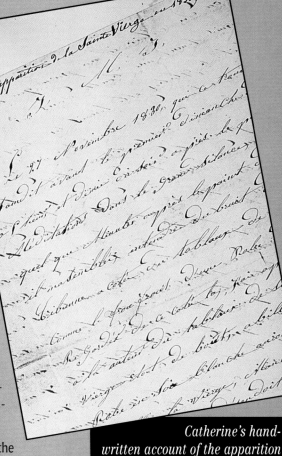

farther these rays spread the larger they became. They caused a great light which was so bright that I could no longer see her feet.

At the same moment that I saw this, the Blessed Virgin lowered her eyes and looked at me. I seemed to hear a voice saying: This globe that you see represents the entire world, especially France, and each person in particular. I do not know how to express how I felt, or how to describe the beauty and grace of what I saw, especially the rays which were so beautiful... This is the symbol of the graces that I pour out upon those who ask for them.' I understood this to mean that the Blessed Virgin desired that people pray to her. She joyfully granted those graces asked of her... At this moment I was filled with rejoicing, and I was not aware of my surroundings.

A sort of oval picture formed around Our Lady. At the top of this image written in gold were the words: 'O Mary conceived without sin, pray for us who have recourse to you.' Then I heard a voice which said, 'Have a medal made according to this model. Everyone who wears it around their neck will receive great graces. For those who wear it with confidence there will be abundant graces.'

Several moments later, the tableau was turned around to reveal the reverse side. Catherine saw the letter M surmounting a small cross. At its base were the sacred hearts of Jesus and Mary.

Catherine's hand-written account of the apparition of November 27

169

Tableau painted in 1855 by the artist Lecerf.

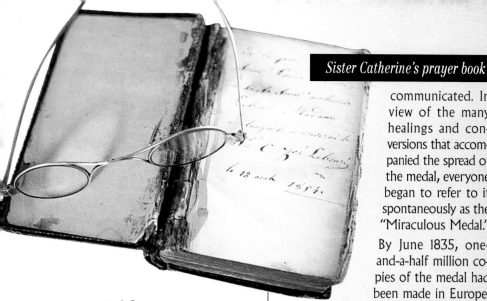

Life at the hospice of Enghien

On February 5, 1831, Sister Catherine Laboure arrived at the hospice of Enghien. This establishment had been founded by the Duchess de Bourbon in memory of her son, the Duke d'Enghien who was executed in 1804 by order of Napoleon I. At first located on the rue de Varenne, in 1828 the establishment was transferred to the rue de Picpus in the Reuilly neighborhood. The hospice housed the retired servants of the royal house of Orleans.

Sister Catherine first was assigned to the kitchen to help the sister-cook. They prepared meals each day for the 50 retirees, the chaplain, the janitor, the gardener, and seven sisters. Her experience working in her brother's restaurant proved to be very useful. However, Catherine suffered from the frugality of her companions. She would have loved to prepare tasty meals for the elderly! During these difficult years her lively temperament was put to the test.

In 1832, an epidemic of cholera ravaged Paris for several months. Thousands died. At the hospice, one of the sisters died. In July, Father Aladel sent the sisters copies of the Medal which he had commissioned to be made by Monsieur Vachette a well-known jeweler. Catherine received her medal in silence. The Daughters of Charity distributed the medal everywhere. They knew that the medal had been made at the request of the Blessed Virgin, but they did not know to whom this message had been communicated. In view of the many healings and conversions that accompanied the spread of the medal, everyone began to refer to it spontaneously as the "Miraculous Medal."

By June 1835, one-and-a-half million copies of the medal had been made in Europe. Catherine thanked Mary in her heart for the rapid spread of this devotion. Father Aladel decided to anonymously publish a small book explaining the origin of this medal. However, he respected Catherine's wish to remain anonymous. During that same year, the artist Lecerf executed two paintings representing *"the apparitions of Mary to Sister X."*

Sister Catherine was now in charge of the section for the retired men. The testimonies of all her Sister companions are unanimous: Catherine loved the men, but could be firm with them when it was necessary. Sister Josephine Combes who spent fifteen years with Sister Catherine recalled:

"I remember that one of the old men got drunk once when he went out. When he returned, Sister Catherine scolded him, but without anger. When one of us criticized her for not being firmer she responded: 'This is because, in spite of everything, I see the Lord in him.' She was right, at that moment, the man was not in a position to profit from her correction. The next day, Sister Catherine talked to the man about his behavior and when he tried to apologize, she replied, 'You need not apologize to me, but to the Good Lord.'"

Sister Rose Charvier (who lived with Sister Catherine for 18 years) gave similar testimony.

"In working with the old men she was very just, and if by chance she had any favorites they were those who were the most ill-tempered and disagreeable. There was an old man who was particularly ornery. He was a real demon, and believed in nothing. Sister Catherine paid him particular attention. Others pointed this out to her. I also did: 'Well, Sister Catherine, your devil is quite unpleasant!' At this, her eyes filled with tears and she was only able to say: 'Yes, please pray for him.'

Sister Angelique Tanguy came to Reuilly in 1863 and was also very struck by Sister Catherine's dedication.

"When the old men were at the point of death, she never left them. Day and night she prayed fervently, had them receive the sacraments, and prepared them for death."

Her responsibility for the old men did not stop Catherine from also taking charge of the hospice's little farm. To the chickens and rabbits, she added cows, and pigeons like she had once tended on her family farm. She guarded the garden from the urchins of the neighborhood who always were trying to steal its pro-

duce. The best of the garden's harvest was reserved for the elderly residents. Sister Marie-Thomas who helped Sister Catherine recalled:

"I asked her permission to have some of the fruit. She told me: 'Ah, my dear sister this fruit is for the elderly. If there is any left you may have some.' I knew there would never be any left."

In 1841, Father Aladel was contemplating having a statue of the Virgin with the globe made as Sister Catherine had often requested at Mary's behest. He asked her to write her recollections of this apparition. On the feast of the Assumption (August 15) Catherine sat down to write the account. She asked Mary for her assistance.

"Today is the feast of the Assumption of the Blessed Virgin Mary. O Queen who is seated before God listen favorably to my prayers. I ask you to give me the strength and the courage to judge what will be for your greater glory."

If her handwriting was poor and her spelling defective, her memory was neither. How could anyone forget the details of such an event? A statue "of the Virgin with the globe" was later made, but it was not as Catherine had described it. This defective statue always bothered her.

In 1842, the remarkable conversion of a young Jewish banker, Alphonse Ratisbonne, took place in Rome. Out of politeness he had agreed to wear a Miraculous Medal which was the gift of a friend. Driven by some force he did not understand, he entered the church of Sant' Andrea delle Fratte. Mary appeared to him there in the same manner in which she was depicted on the medal. *"She did not say anything to me, but I understood everything."* When he arrived in France, Alphonse Ratisbonne asked to meet the sister who first had the joy of seeing Mary. Catherine preferred to remain anonymous.

Sister Stephanie Cosnard who lived at Reuilly for nine years, and who often saw Sister Catherine at the mother house was a witness to her profound humility:

"Her humility consisted of a complete self-forgetfulness, and a great personal simplicity. She loved to humble herself in front of everyone. I also believe that it was this profound feeling of humility which motivated her throughout her life to keep silent about the extraordinary favors granted her by God and the Blessed Virgin... Other sisters may have been more perfect than her in exterior things, but none of them could match her total abandonment to the love of God and of the Blessed Virgin, or her total self-detachment."

The Reuilly neighborhood contained numerous paper factories staffed with many child laborers. Struck hard by the recession in France between 1846 and 1848, the adult workers participated in the Revolution of 1848. The hospice at Reuilly welcomed and cared for the wounded of both sides as was done by Sister Rosalie Rendu in the Mouffetard neighborhood.

Following the upheavals caused by another cholera epidemic, a small orphanage and then a school were opened for the orphans of this poor neighborhood. The community of sisters grew. The thirty sisters were divided into two groups. One served the elderly of the hospice, and the other served the children in the new home called

The garden of the Enghien hospice

Holy Mary's Providence. All the sisters prayed together. For seventeen years, Sister Philomene Millon sat next to Sister Catherine. She never forgot her countenance:

"Her faith was very lively. One could see this especially when we were in the chapel. When I, as a young sister, arrived at the Enghien house I was struck by her. During the time of prayer she remained immobile with her eyes fixed on the statue of the Blessed Virgin. I still think of this when I see the place that she occupied. At that time, I had no inkling that she had been the one honored in such an extraordinary way by the Blessed Virgin. There was nothing about her that set her apart from any of the other sisters."

Later in life, Sister Catherine was assigned to spend most of the day minding the front door and receiving visitors, or the poor who were seeking assistance. Sister Anne-Marie Levacher was happy to have had the opportunity to recite the rosary with her:

"Sometimes I went to recite the rosary with Sister Catherine in the reception area where she worked. There was a little statue of the Blessed Virgin there. I loved to say the rosary with her. I was always edified by the way she recited it."

Over the subsequent fifty years there were three events that gladdened Sister Catherine's heart. As Mary had requested on the night of July 18, 1830, the Association of the Children of Mary was founded. On November 21, 1851 the Association was established at Reuilly. Catherine's niece, Tonine's daughter, joined this association in 1857, to her aunt's great satisfaction.

The second event was prepared for by the worldwide diffusion of more than 100 million Miraculous Medals inscribed with the prayer *"O Mary, conceived without sin, pray for us who have recourse to you."* On December 8, 1854, Pope Pius IX defined the dogma of the Immaculate Conception.

Four years later at Lourdes, a young shepherdess received a visit from a "beautiful lady." When asked her name the mysterious lady responded: "I am the Immaculate Conception."

When Catherine heard of the apparition at Lourdes she said. *"This is the same woman."* The memory of these two visionaries made indelible impressions on all those who saw them. Father Hamard, a French Vincentian, wrote these words after the death of Bernadette Soubirous:

"She was very small, pale, and shy. Her eyes shone with a marvelous brightness. I had seen nothing like them except at the hospice at Enghien in 1876."

If the messenger of Lourdes was well known, the one from the rue du Bac remained unknown. However, in the books written about the Miraculous Medal it was said that the sister who had seen the Blessed Mother in 1830 had been a novice at the time. In later years, the number of sisters who had made their novitiate that year grew smaller through deaths. Little-by-little, attention turned toward Sister Catherine. She did all she could to avoid this unwelcome notice. There are many testimonies about this. Sister Rose recalled what she had heard:

"When I was in the novitiate at the mother house in 1855, many sisters told me: 'The sister who saw the Blessed Virgin is now taking

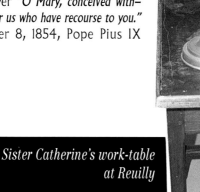

care of cows in a house somewhere near Paris.' When I was sent to the house at Enghien I shared this work with Sister Catherine. I told myself then, 'No, it could not be her. I did not find her mystical enough.'"

Catherine's niece, Marie-Antoinette, also doubted that the recipient could have been her aunt:

"I recall that when at age eighteen I was received into the Children of Mary by Father Aladel... my aunt was overjoyed that I was the first member of the family to become a member. In 1859, a friend showed me a booklet about the Miraculous Medal. It said that the Blessed Virgin had appeared to a Sister "L." This friend told me: "Perhaps it was your aunt." I responded: "I would be astonished if this were true. She has never spoken to me about this. There are other sisters whose last name begins with L."

In 1875, Sister Catherine dealt with some imprudent remarks made by another sister:

"The Count and Countess d'Avenel came to visit. Sister Catherine was on duty and opened the door. I said in a low voice to the countess: 'This is the Sister who had the vision of the Medal.' The Countess told her husband this, and he turned around and said to Sister Catherine: 'Sister, I am honored to be in the presence of the sister who has seen the Blessed Virgin.' I said to the Countess, 'What has your husband done!' Sister Catherine seemed stunned, and pretended not to have heard what was said. A little later, Sister Catherine spoke to our superior asking her to be stricter with the young sisters like me. I went to apologize to her. Sister Catherine told me clearly but kindly, 'My dear, it was wrong to speak in this way to outsiders.'"

If Sister Catherine did not like to be spoken about, she also could not tolerate any-

The "Catherine Laboure Retirement Home" on the rue de Reuilly

one questioning the apparition of Our Lady. Sister Angelique Tanguy once witnessed her reaction to this:

"We were gathered for recreation in the parlor, working and talking. A young sister said: 'This Sister who was supposed to have seen the Blessed Virgin undoubtedly only saw a painting or something similar.' Then, Sister Catherine who usually spoke very little, raised her eyes and said in a very firm voice: 'My dear, the Sister who saw the Blessed Virgin saw her as clearly as I am seeing you.' Then she continued with her work."

On July 19, 1870, Emperor Napoleon III declared war on Prussia. The war went badly for France. On September 18, the Prussians laid siege to Paris. The winter was hard with many wounded and starving. After the peace treaty was signed a civil war broke out in the capital. The rebels attacked everything religious. Easter evening they invaded the house

Statue of the Virgin in the garden at Enghien

at Reuilly and tried to seize the superior as prisoner. The sisters resisted. Sister Dufes was obliged to flee Paris. Eventually, all the sisters including Catherine would have to leave until after the civil war was put down.

If Sister Catherine did not experience any additional visions of the Virgin after 1830 she still was in communication with her. Mary had asked that a statue be erected depicting her holding the world in her hands. Father Aladel did not do this before his death in 1865. Being seventy years old, Sister Catherine sensed the end of her own life approaching. She wanted to meet with the new director, Father Jules Chinchon. Who would take her there? She prayed to Mary, and asked to meet with her superior. The next day she spent two hours recounting the details of all the apparitions to Sister Jeanne Dufes. She insisted that the statue of Mary holding the world between her hands be made as quickly as possible.

After hearing this, Sister Dufes knelt down to ask Sister Catherine's forgiveness for having treated her so harshly at times. She said:

"You have been highly favored."

Sister Catherine responded with great humility:

"Oh! I have only been an instrument. The Blessed Virgin did not appear on my behalf... If the Blessed Virgin chose me who knew nothing, it was so that no one could doubt her."

During the summer of 1876 an artist made the statue of the Virgin as Catherine had requested. She would be very disappointed with the result.

In November, Sister Catherine's health declined. She could no longer leave her room. She told those around her that she would not live to see the new year. She asked to receive the sacrament of the sick. All of the community was there praying with her. On December 31, at 7:00 p.m. Catherine quietly died. Her face was radiant. Sister Dufes told the sisters, "Yes, it is true that she was the one who saw the Blessed Virgin."

The community wanted her body to rest at Reuilly in the vault under their chapel. Permission was granted by the government. On January 3, 1877, a long funeral procession entered the garden at Reuilly. Instead of funeral hymns there were hymns of thanksgiving. All those who were there believed they were already honoring a saint who had seen the Virgin Mary, and who for forty-six years had been a simple servant of Jesus Christ in the poor. Catherine Laboure was canonized July 27, 1947.

Photograph of Sister Catherine taken shortly before her death

The shrine of Saint Catherine Laboure

On January 3, 1877, the body of Catherine Laboure was laid to rest in the crypt of the chapel at Reuilly. Her remains were interred there until the time of her beatification.

On March 21, 1933, Catherine's tomb was opened and her body was exhumed. The witnesses to this event included representatives from the Archdiocese of Paris, the Daughters of Charity, the Congregation of the Mission, and medical experts. To everyone's great astonishment, when the coffin was opened, the body of Sister Catherine was found to be incorrupt.

After a detailed examination, the body was taken to the mother house of the Daughters of Charity in Paris. A large group of Vincentians and Daughters of Charity were on hand for this solemn and prayerful occasion.

The next day, the archbishop of Paris, Cardinal Verdier addressed the Daughters of Charity and Vincentians who had gathered at the motherhouse in the presence of the remains of Sister Catherine: *"It is infinitely more important that you endeavor to keep Catherine's spirit rather than just watch over her remains. I believe that you now have among you 'the saint of humility.'"*

A detailed medical examination of Sister Catherine's exhumed remains concluded: *"The body is in a perfect state of preservation, and its joints are still supple."*

After the celebration of her beatification on May 28, 1933, the body of Sister Catherine was placed under the renovated altar honoring the "Virgin of the globe." Thus, countless pilgrims have been able to gather close to her as they pray for her intercession, and that of the Blessed Virgin.

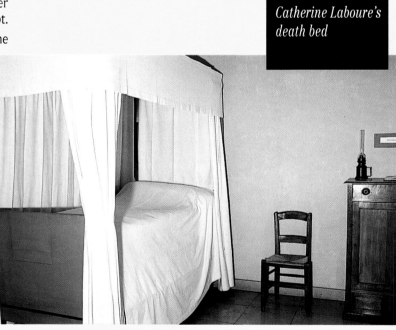

Catherine Laboure's death bed

Tombstone in the crypt at Reuilly

MAUREJEAN

VIRGINI IMMACULATÆ OB INNUMERABILIA ET
PORTENTOSA BENEFICIA HOC ALTARE ÆDIFICAVIT GRATITUDO

O Mary, conceived without sin, pray for us who have recourse to you.

O Mary, conceived without sin, pray for us who have recourse to you.
O Mary, this was the prayer that you gave to Saint Catherine Laboure
in the Chapel of the Apparitions, more than one hundred and fifty years ago;
This invocation, engraved on the Miraculous Medal,
is now worn and repeated by the faithful throughout the world.

Blessed are you among women!
You are intimately associated with the work of our Redemption,
associated with the Cross of our Savior,
your heart has been pierced, next to his heart.
And now, in the glory of your Son,
you never cease to intercede for us, poor sinners.

You watch over the Church for you are its Mother.
You watch over each of your Children.
From God, you obtain for us,
all the graces that are symbolized by the rays of light
which radiate from your open hands,
and the only condition that you demand of us
is that we approach
with the confidence, the hardiness, and the simplicity of a child.

And it is thus that you bring us before your Divine Son.

John Paul II (1980)

178

Prayer of Saint

Catherine Labouré

Whenever I go to the chapel,
I put myself in the presence of our good Lord, and I say to him
"Lord, I am here.
Tell me what you would have me do."

If he gives me some task,
I am content and I thank him.

If he gives me nothing,
I still thank him
since I do not deserve to receive anything more than that.

And then, I tell God
everything that is in my heart.
I tell him about my pains and my joys,
and then I listen.

If you listen, God will also speak to you,
for with the good Lord, you have to both speak and listen.

God always speaks to you
when you approach him plainly and simply.

of the Apparitions

by Father René Coste

*Honorary Professor of the Faculty of Theology, Catholic Institute of Toulouse,
President of Pax Christi, France*

An Interpretation

A.

The Apparitions

(April-December 1830)

In order to understand the message communicated to Catherine Laboure, it is necessary to consider the apparitions as a whole: that of the heart of Saint Vincent, the apparitions of Our Lord in the Eucharist, and those of the Blessed Virgin.

The heart
of Saint Vincent
(April 25 - May 2)

The "vision of the heart" which was repeated for three successive days is of enormous significance. This is particularly true in light of the interpretation of its colors, given by the recipient herself.

According to Catherine, the appearance of the *"white"* heart, *"symbolized peace, calm, innocence, and unity."* These four words complement and clarify each other, and none should be overlooked. From the point of view of Biblical theology, the first color holds a privileged position. According to the Old and New Testaments, peace is the essential characteristic of the messianic age. It is God's greatest gift to humanity transmitted through the risen Christ. The peace that God gives us, and which he wills should exist between us, calls us to create lines of communication, cooperation and reconciliation with our brothers and sisters. According to the letter to the Ephesians (6:15), the good news of peace is the synthesis of divine revelation.

The *"symbol of fire"* according to Catherine *"represents the charity that must illumine our hearts."* In human history, fire is one of the great symbols of the presence and activity of God. (For example the "flaming fire" on Mount Horeb (Ex 3:1-6); the "tongues as of fire" of Pentecost (Acts 2-3). There are also the words of Jesus, *"I have come to light a fire on the earth. How I wish the blaze were ignited!"* (Lk 12:49)

According to the visionary, the purpose of this divine fire is to illumine charity in human hearts. At the heart of revelation is the belief that God is "Love" (1 Jn 4:8). God reveals the fullness of his tenderness for humanity in his beloved Son who gives his life for the salvation of the world, and who makes "Love" of God and of neighbor the great commandment that he gives to his disciples.

The young visionary was a zealous daughter of Saint Vincent de Paul. She so admired him that she prayed to be able to imitate him by consecrating her life to the service of the poor. She understood that above all the poor need to be loved. Only in the heart of God can one find the energy to sustain an intense love and a life-long dedication to the service of the poor.

Catherine understood that the Company of the Daughters of Charity needed *"to undergo a renewal."* This apostolic renewal had to take place if it was to *"extend itself to the farthest reaches of the world."* This expansion in turn would enable it to testify everywhere to its legacy of love of the poor given it by Saint Vincent de Paul. A universal dimension appears in all the apparitions. This is the underlying theme of Mary's message.

With regard to the meaning of the symbolism of the color *"black"* this color is commonly thought to indicate misfortune and suffering. *"The heart of Saint Vincent is profoundly afflicted by the misfortunes happening in France."* Historically, one could interpret this as a concern with the revolutionary troubles of 1830, 1848, and 1871. But this apparition is not time-bound. A sensibility to the trials of humanity, and the invitation to a profound compassion, are also key elements of Mary's message.

The apparitions of Our Lord in the Eucharist

The Eucharist is at the heart of the mystery of the Christian Faith. In fulfillment of Jesus's promise, *"Know that I am with you always, until the end of the world!"* (Mt 28:20). The Eucharist is the sacrament which signifies with the greatest force the presence of the Risen One at the heart of the Church and of humanity.

How are Saint Catherine's apparitions of Our Lord related to this sacrament? She said, *"During the entire time that I was in the novitiate I saw... Our Lord in the Blessed Sacrament."* She also recalled that on June 6, the Feast of the Holy Trinity, the crucified Lord appeared to her *"in the Blessed Sacrament as a King,"* *"stripped of all his ornaments."*

The visionary had the interior sense that this vision identified the crucified and risen Jesus with all those who suffered, with all the victims of misery, exploitation, and oppression, throughout the world. This would be in accordance with the words of the King, the Sovereign Judge of humanity, spoken in the Last Judgment (Mt 25:31-36).

The apparitions of the Blessed Virgin

The apparition of July 18, 1830

In the course of this first apparition, the Blessed Virgin revealed to Catherine that she would *"be given a mission"* which would cause her great trials: *"You will experience pain... torment... and contradiction."* Following the example of Jesus Christ, vocations to God's service generally involve great trials. This was confirmed in the prophecy of Simeon to Mary: *"you yourself shall be pierced with a sword"* (Lk 2:35).

The Blessed Virgin twice told Catherine, *"do not fear."* These words echo God's frequent biblical exhortations "to have confidence." He gave this encouragement to those to whom he had entrusted a mission. These words *"do not fear,"* also were echoed by John Paul II at the beginning of his pontificate. They are an appeal to faith, and courage, in difficult times. *"You will receive the grace you need, said the Blessed Virgin... have confidence."*

Mary continued her message to Catherine telling her in great detail of the misfortunes that would befall France and the world: *"The entire world will experience misfortunes of all sorts... the entire world will be engulfed in sad-*

ness." She also spoke about bloody religious persecution: *"The cross will be scorned... the streets will be filled with blood..."*

What is interesting here, in terms of a theological and pastoral reflection, is again the universal perspective of this message given the terrible violence and suffering experienced by humanity.

The visionary was called to identify with and pray for this suffering humanity: *"Come to the foot of this altar. Here, graces will be spread over all those who ask for them with confidence and fervor: the great and the small."* It is not only to Catherine that this message was addressed, but to all those who through her become aware of this message. This is a pressing invitation to pray for all humanity in the midst of its sufferings and trials. This is a pressing invitation to pray that humanity will undergo the conversion that will make it more just and loving. And how can it be forgotten that Christian prayer is a radical call to personal action, so that we will be inspired to do all that we can so that the world will come to resemble the world that we pray for?

The Apparitions of November 27, and December 1830

The apparition of the Blessed Virgin in December does not seem to have any importance from a theological point of view. She appeared again as she had appeared in the second vision, which is the one of decisive importance. In this vision, she concretized the mission confided to Catherine by means of a medal so original and so rich in its symbolism that one can only call it the "Miraculous Medal."

The woman who appeared to Catherine possessed an inexpressible beauty. She was resplendent because she reflected the beauty of God. This beauty was the same glory that transformed Christ in the Transfiguration. This same glory one day will be reflected on the faces of all those who rise from the dead, and is reflected now "as in a mirror" (1 Cor 15:43), on the faces of the living.

The meditation on God's beauty and the grace of the beauty that he accords to the lives of the saints is one of the great traditions of Eastern Christian spirituality and theology. In the revelation of the medal, the beauty which transfigures the face of Mary and *"the rays of ravishing beauty"* which emanate from her hands, constitute one of the greatest expressions of God's beauty in the Western Christian tradition. The rays take on even more significance when they are seen as *"the symbol of the graces that Mary obtains for humanity."*

Catherine saw this marvelous vision of beauty surrounded by the words written in gold: *"O Mary, conceived without sin, pray for us who have recourse to you."* As a little

later at Lourdes, this invocation is dedicated to Mary as the Immaculate Conception, and is an important manifestation of Marian devotion for Catholicism in the 19th century. The Second Vatican Council appealed to this rich devotional tradition when it said: "It was a custom already established by the Holy Fathers to call the Mother of God, the all holy, preserved from all stain of sin, having been touched by the Holy Spirit, and formed as a new creation. She was enriched

from the first moment of her conception with a brilliant, absolutely unique holiness."

At this point in the vision, the picture reversed itself. Catherine then saw the letter M surmounted by a small cross, having at its base the Sacred Hearts of Jesus and Mary. This last phase of the vision is of great importance.

This symbolism identifies Mary completely with Christ the Redeemer as his

Mother and as the Servant of the Lord (Lk 1:38). It identifies her as the one who constantly lived in the light of the Word of God (Lk 2:23). She instructed the servants at the wedding in Cana, and through them her son's disciples through all ages, *"Do whatever he tells you,"* (Jn 2:5). The vision reaffirmed the power of Mary's intercession. But it is clearly revealed as an "intercession": the intercession of a Mother as at Cana, and the intercession of a servant which she always desired to be.

During the first apparition Mary said that her heavenly mission was *"to give glory to the good God."* She used this expression to explain to Catherine the mission she would confide to her. If, as in this message, the Glory of God is reflected upon Mary, it is then through her intercession, and her advocacy that humanity discovers and comes to love the God who is Love. Mary is thus an evangelizer par excellence.

The Medal serves as an icon for the poor. It is most often made from a common and inexpensive metal, and costs next to nothing. Anyone can possess one.

Choosing to wear the medal expresses a person's confidence in, and attachment for, the woman who is our Mother in the order of grace. When we as sons and daughters accept this medal as her gift it is a gesture that strengthens the bonds of a family's love.

As human beings, we have need of signs and symbols in our lives. The incomparable popularity and success of the Miraculous Medal as a sign and symbol of our faith illustrates this fact. Marian devotion is one of the great foundations of the Christian spiritual tradition. Mary, according to the New Testament, is intimately connected to the mysteries of the Incarnation and the Redemption. As God's gift to humanity, Mary also provides a pathway leading back to God.

The Miraculous Medal, seen in light of Mary's message to Catherine Laboure is a path to evangelization. This symbol reveals a message that can only be understood by being put into practice.

The witness and her times

The witness

At the time of the apparitions, Catherine Laboure was preparing to become a member of a religious community which dedicated itself, in a spirit of evangelical charity, to the service of the poor.

One must always avoid the tendency of limiting the significance of Catherine's life to the fact that she was a sister. Every vocation to the service of God and neighbor should find inspiration in her example. In addition, as Rene Laurentin has observed, "she appears as the first example of a new type of sanctity that the Holy Spirit began to raise up in modern times: a sanctity without external glory, or great human triumphs. Above all Catherine received the grace of fulfilling, with great holiness, the ordinary tasks of her daily routine. What was important to her was her service of the poor."

The Blessed Virgin herself is the first model for this type of sanctity.

Catherine, who was a young woman when she witnessed the apparitions of 1830, subsequently led a life which remains as an example to young people. This example urges young people to choose, in the words of the Book of Deuteronomy (Dt 30:15-20) "life and goodness," and not "death and dishonor." Her life serves an example of the dynamism of active charity, equilibrium in life, and the saintliness possible in one's everyday existence.

That fact that the witness to the apparitions was a woman also reflects the inherent dignity and vocation of women in the Church and society. This is discussed by Pope John Paul II in his 1988 apostolic letter *"Mulieris dignitatem."*

The era

The period from 1815 to 1871 saw the height of the industrial revolution and capitalism in France and most other developed countries. This was also an age of great poverty and despair. The life of workers and their families was terribly hard. Modern social welfare benefits were practically non-existent. Industrial capitalism reshaped the world. Certainly, this resulted in the improvement of material life for a large part of human society, but this "progress" was at the cost of great suffering for the poor and working classes.

When God chose Mary to be his messenger to this young woman, and later to the adolescent Bernadette, he was indicating his stance against misery, and against massive injustice in the world.

In addition, it should not be forgotten that a process of dechristianization began in the 19th century and was progressively engulfing all Western Europe.

The Marian apparitions of 1830 issue a call to prayer, faith, and charity, which must be seen within this historical context.

The place

Another important aspect to consider with regards to the apparitions of 1830 is where they took place; namely, in the middle of one of the greatest cities in the world: a political, cultural and economic capital. All the other Marian apparitions of the 19th and 20th centuries took place in the countryside (Lourdes, Knock, Fatima, La Salette). This characteristic surely merits further reflection.

The dogma of the Immaculate Conception

by Cardinal Jacques Martin

On December 8, 1854 the dogma of the Immaculate Conception of the Virgin Mary was solemnly defined by Pope Pius IX.

A contested truth

That this solemn article of our faith was only relatively recently defined can lead one to ask, why did it take eighteen centuries to proclaim the existence of a truth contained in Christian revelation?

The explanation for this situation can be found in the fact that in the course of the history of the Church, the Immaculate Conception had been the object of some disagreement. The sources of these disagreements were twofold. The first was the universality of original sin taught with such vigor by Saint Paul in his letters, and the universality of Redemption in which it seemed impossible to exempt one sole creature, even if she was the Mother of God.

The Council of Trent shed light on this first point when it declared that it did not intend "to include the Blessed and Immaculate Virgin Mary in the decree relative to original sin."

With regard to the second point, theologians introduced the distinction between the Redemption of the victims of original sin and the antecedent "preservation" accorded to the Virgin Mary in view of the future Redemption.

Despite these reservations, the feast of the Immaculate Conception spread gradually throughout the Church.

The Medal and the Chapel of the Apparitions

In the course of the 19th century, an event took place to which historians have not attached enough significance. This occurrence greatly contributed to the spread of this devotion. This event was the mission confided by the Blessed Virgin in 1830 to a novice of the Daughters of Charity in Paris, the future Saint Catherine Laboure. In the course of an apparition Mary said, *"Have a medal made based on this model. All those who wear it will receive great graces."* The model portrayed the Virgin Mary with her hands extended emitting rays of light, together with the inscription: *"O Mary, conceived without sin, pray for us who have recourse to you."*

It took Catherine Laboure a while to persuade her confessor about the authenticity of this message, and because of political conditions it took a while for the confessor to get permission from the archbishop of Paris. Finally, in 1832, the first medals were made. These were soon distributed throughout France, and then throughout Europe and the world. They were accompanied by a profusion of healings and conversions so that soon the medal commonly was referred to as the "Miraculous Medal."

Rene Laurentin has studied these events with the precision of a historian. He has concluded that in the course of the ten years between 1832 and 1842 more then 100 million Miraculous Medals were distributed. Throughout the world, millions of voices repeated the prayerful invocation *"O Mary, conceived without sin, pray for us who have recourse to you."* Laurentin does not hesitate to describe this phenomenon "as one of the greatest examples of social communication prior to the birth of modern telecommunications."

The first decade of the medal's existence ended with a spectacular miracle in 1842. A young Jewish man was visiting Rome. He was engaged to be married, and any thoughts of religion were far from his mind. A Catholic friend had given him a Miraculous Medal, which out of courtesy he was wearing around his neck. Accompanying his friend on a visit to the church of Sant'Andrea delle Fratte he saw the Virgin Mary exactly as she appeared on the medal. Struck by this apparition he requested to be baptized, and later was ordained a priest. The young man's name was Alphonse Ratisbonne.

In light of these developments one can better understand why during the pontificate of Gregory XVI (1831-1846) a large number of bishops asked the Pope to define the Immaculate Conception as a dogma of the faith.

The definition of 1854

At the beginning of his pontificate, Pius IX named a commission of twenty theologians to study the question of whether the Immaculate Conception was definable as a truth of the Faith. On February 2, 1849, he asked all the bishops of the world for their opinions concerning the definability of the Immaculate Conception. He received almost 600 responses, of these 550 were favorable, only 50 were negative or uncertain. Pius IX continued the consultations and study.

Finally, on December 8, 1854, the dogmatic definition took place at Saint Peter's basilica in Rome before 200 cardinals, archbishops, bishops and an immense gathering of the faithful.

"From the first moment of her conception, by the grace and privilege of God the all powerful, and in consideration of the merits of Jesus Christ, the Savior of humanity, the Virgin Mary was preserved intact from the stain of original sin. This is the faith of the Catholic Church."

This theological initiative of Pius IX elicited a favorable response from the entire Catholic world. When the Cure of Ars heard the news he was said to have declared, "Oh how wonderful! I have always thought that the light of Catholic truth lacked the brilliance of this ray."

The response of heaven at Lourdes

This dogmatic definition also received a heavenly confirmation unique in the history of the Church.

Less than four years later, word began to spread that in a village in the Pyrenees, an innocent young girl named Bernadette, had received visits from and been given tasks by a "mysterious" lady. At first, the local pastor doubted the girl's story. He asked the young girl, *"What did the Lady say her name was?"* Bernadette answered, *"When I asked her, she only smiled and said nothing."*

Finally, near the end of the apparitions, Bernadette had the courage again to ask the Lady to tell her who she was. This time she received the response that amazed the entire Church: *"I am the Immaculate Conception."* These words had no meaning to Bernadette, but they did to the local pastor. He no longer doubted the sincerity of Bernadette who could not have invented these words that she did not understand. Nor did he doubt the identity of the mysterious "Lady."

In saying *"I am the Immaculate Conception,"* Mary thus highlighted the nature of her privilege. There was only one Immaculate Conception. There had never been another one, nor would there ever be another one.

With the authorization of Lourdes Magazine, excerpted from an article of March 25, 1990

Come to the foot of this altar.

> At the Chapel of the Apparitions, as elsewhere, Mary revealed herself as the evangelizer par excellence: *"Come to the foot of this altar."*

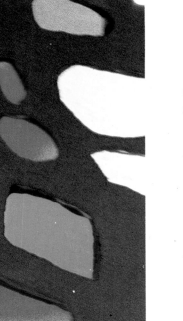

Jesus present in the Eucharist

By pointing to the altar, Mary invited Catherine and us through her, to encounter Jesus present in the Eucharist.

Mary encourages us to, first of all, have the attitude of confident humility that is necessary in order to encounter her Son in the Eucharist. *"These graces will be spread over all those who ask for them with confidence and fervor."*

By virtue of this promise, Mary also forcefully reminds us, that in our life, there are privileged meeting places that will be life-giving for us: prayer and the Eucharist. Thus, the first duty of a Christian is to come regularly to the place where Jesus shares his love with his friends.

The mystery of Christ the servant

The love received by partaking in the Eucharistic meal is designed to strengthen us for service to our neighbor. Mary reminded us of this when she indicated that it was at the foot of the altar that we would learn to enter into the mystery of the servant Christ.

Jesus established the Eucharist the same day that he washed the feet of his disciples. On the eve of giving his life out of love for humanity, Jesus the Lord and Master, made himself a servant. He thus indicated the value of humble service and invited his friends to follow his example as an expression of true love: *"As I have done. So you must do"* (Jn 13:13-17).

In leading us to discover the mystery of Christ, the servant of the Father and of his brothers and sisters, Mary encourages us to always discover that the consequence and the fullest expression of the Eucharist is service to our neighbor.

In 1962, the Second Vatican Council reaffirmed the Church's obligation to be a servant, and thus for each of its members to be a servant. *"Under the inspiration of the Spirit, the consoler, the Church has only one purpose, to continue the work of Christ, who came into the world to testify to the truth, to save and not to condemn, to serve and not be served."* (Gaudium et Spes)

Because the temptation to power and selfishness are always present somewhere in our hearts, possessing the attitude of a servant does not come naturally to us. Rather, this evangelical attitude is a gift of God, a grace one must ask to receive each day.

Thus, it is not difficult to understand why Mary, our Mother, the humble servant invites us "to come to the foot of the altar." Here in our communion with the servant Christ, we learn to become what we receive as we serve our brothers and sisters. When this communion is achieved, justice and love will flourish in our world.